Plagiarism: A How-Not-To Guide for Students

Plagiarism: A How-Not-To Guide for Students

Barry Gilmore

HEINEMANN
Portsmouth, NH

Heinemann
361 Hanover Street
Portsmouth, NH 03801–3912
www.heinemann.com

Offices and agents throughout the world

Library of Congress Cataloging-in-Publication Data
Gilmore, Barry.
   Plagiarism : a how-not-to guide for students / Barry Gilmore.
      p. cm.
   Includes bibliographical references and index.
   ISBN-13: 978-0-325-02643-5
   ISBN-10: 0-325-02643-2
   1. Plagiarism—Prevention.   2. Student ethics.   I. Title.

PN167.G46 2009
371.5'8—dc22   2008048850

Editor: Lisa Luedeke
Production editor: Sonja S. Chapman
Cover design: Night & Day Design
Compositor: Kim Arney
Manufacturing: Steve Bernier

Printed in the United States of America on acid-free paper
13 12 11 10 09 VP   2 3 4 5

Contents

1 *Introduction*

Taking the Plague Out of Plagiarism

Plagiarism is easy.

There's no sugarcoating the fact that if you want to cheat on a written assignment, you can find a way, and it will take you less time and effort (unless you get caught) than writing an original paper would. Back when your parents and teachers were in high school, plagiarism wasn't such a snap—if they wanted to plagiarize a report on, say, the migratory habits of mosquito larvae, they had to trudge to the library, actually *find* a source on mosquitoes using an old-fashioned card catalog (no easy trick), and then copy out the information by *hand* onto sheets of notebook paper. What a pain, right? Today you google "mosquito larvae" and "migration," click a couple of keys, and cut and paste the information from www.mosquitoes .org right into a Word document. What could be simpler?

Of course, getting caught is easy, too. Search engines like Google and Yahoo! make it easier than ever for teachers to find plagiarized material; I often don't have to search more than one time, using one phrase, to find the Web location of borrowed material students include in their papers. Add to that the existence of search detection services like Turnitin.com (with that site, I don't even have to type to search for material online; I can make *students* submit the papers for me and the search results come back to me) and the quest to hunt down plagiarized papers becomes easier than ever.

Avoiding plagiarism, though—that's sometimes tough to do. I don't mean, of course, that you, as a student, are somehow hardwired to cheat at every given opportunity. Most students—at least most I've worked with—agree that wholesale copying is usually wrong and that writing original work is, in the long run, a good idea. So the book you're holding doesn't aim to moralize about what's fundamentally right or wrong, or to insult you by offering advice that's pretty obvious to most students. It also doesn't aim to excuse plagiarism or to remove the responsibility you have for making sure work is your own.

This book aims to help you avoid plagiarism by offering better alternatives.

In fact, I believe that there's a problem with the whole line of thinking I just introduced, the thinking that begins with *plagiarism is easy* and ends with *getting caught is easy, too, so don't do it*. The problem arises when someone assumes that all students plagiarize simply because it's easy to do so or because they're just dishonest twerps (even if that's sometimes the case). And actually, that assumption isn't one that's made only by teachers. Most students I speak with think that plagiarism happens mostly for just those reasons. As you'll see in a chart that appears in the next chapter, about a quarter of the students at the school where I teach think that plagiarism happens mainly because it's easy or because students are plain lazy.

The problem continues when we assume that it's a teacher's job to catch and stop plagiarism. Sure, teachers don't like cheating. But when a teacher has to spend time chasing down copied work, both the teacher and student have already lost valuable time and trust. That means, of course, that your teachers bear some responsibility, not to make sure that you don't plagiarize, but to help make sure that you don't *want* to plagiarize. There's a whole teacher edition of this book that addresses ways teachers can change assignments, grading systems, classroom rules, and school culture to help make plagiarism not only unattractive but just plain unnecessary. In the ideal world, plagiarism would still be easy—it just wouldn't happen.

Uh-huh, you say. Right. We don't live in an ideal world. We live in a world—we go to schools—where deadlines pile up, where the importance of grades has been inflated by parents and schools and the college admissions process, where citation formats can seem complicated and pointless, where assignments aren't always clear, where teachers sometimes do assign busywork, where it seems like those who cheat get ahead, where the Internet makes rules of ownership fuzzy and yes, where plagiarism is easy, sometimes *really* easy. You're expected to navigate that world without resorting to cheating or copying others' work, and the bad news is that as plagiarism gets easier, teachers are feeling less and less sympathetic. Search for books and articles on plagiarism online and you'll find titles that include words like *scourge, war, robbery,* and my favorite, *plague* (clever writers love to pull that word out of the term plagiarism, but don't be deceived—their Latin roots aren't the same).

Plagiarism is not a disease. It's not a scourge, and if students and teachers consider it to be a war, it's a war everyone will lose. As I said before, teachers have their part to play in making certain that we avoid combat by making learning a mutual, high-interest, student-centered activity.

You have your part to play, too. It involves knowing what is and isn't considered plagiarism, knowing how to write without plagiarizing, and doing your best to make sure that plagiarism and cheating aren't the most attractive options for your own work. To do that, you've got to think about the causes and consequences of cheating, as well as the benefits of original work, *before* you encounter temptation, confusion, or misunderstandings. That's the purpose of this book: not to accuse you of plagiarizing or to make it sound inevitable that you'll cheat, and not only to give you a way out of a tricky situation well before you need it, but also to help you avoid tricky situations in the first place.

■ CASE STUDY: BLIND JUSTICE?

Consider this: In 1892, when she was twelve years old, Helen Keller (yes, *that* Helen Keller) was accused of plagiarism. The work in question was a story titled "The Frost King," substantial portions of which, it turns out, were copied from a story by nineteenth-century author Margaret T. Canby titled "The Frost Fairies."

In her autobiography, Keller admits to borrowing from another's work:

> At that time I eagerly absorbed everything I read without a thought of authorship, and even now I cannot be quite sure of the boundary line between my ideas and those I find in books. . . . But the fact remains that Miss Canby's story was read to me once, and that long after I had forgotten it, it came back to me so naturally that I never suspected that it was the child of another mind. (1952, 63)

The accusation and subsequent inquisition of Keller by her teachers, along with the realization that she had, in fact, unwittingly plagiarized a story by another writer, shook Keller. She avoided ever writing fiction again and, if we can believe her assertions of innocence, turned to autobiography partly as a way to prove to herself as well as to others her own authorship. Notice how Keller felt when she discovered that she had appropriated another's words:

> The two stories were so much alike in thought and language that it was evident Miss Canby's story had been read to me, and that mine was—a plagiarism. It was difficult to make me understand this; but when I did understand I was astonished and grieved. No child ever drank deeper of the cup of bitterness than I did. I had disgraced myself; I had brought

suspicion upon those I loved best. . . . As I lay in my bed that night, I wept as I hope few children have wept. I felt so cold, I imagined I should die before morning, and the thought comforted me. I think if this sorrow had come to me when I was older, it would have broken my spirit beyond repairing. (1952, 64)

Flash-forward more than a century, to 2006: Keller's story became a hot topic once more, this time for its usefulness as a comparison with the case of a Harvard sophomore, Kaavya Viswanathan, who was accused of plagiarizing material from two young adult novels by Megan McCafferty. Here's an excerpt from a *New York Times* article focusing on the young author:

Under scrutiny, [she] suddenly recalled adoring Ms. McCafferty's books and claimed to have unconsciously channeled them. Given that, her critics charged, she was being treated better than other fabulists of late. . . . But what if she had been deaf and blind? (Zeller 2006)

In other words, the author of this article asks us, would the press today treat Keller and Viswanathan similarly?

For the sake of comparison, look at how Viswanathan explained herself to Katie Couric on the *Today* show:

I completely see the similarities. I'm not denying that those are there, but I can honestly say that any of those similarities were completely unconscious and unintentional, that while I was reading Megan McCafferty's books, I must have just internalized her words. I never, ever intended to deliberately take any of her words. (Schleicher 2006)

Viswanathan's book, incidentally, was withdrawn from stores, and she lost book and movie deals that were potentially worth millions of dollars.

Find Out More

- Check out Helen Keller's autobiography, *The Story of My Life* (1952), from your library or find it for free on the website of the American Foundation for the Blind (www.afb.org/mylife). The entire account of the episode described in this case study can be found in Chapter 14 of the book.

- Type Kaavya Viswanathan's name into an online search engine and you'll find plenty of articles about her. You might wish to visit Wikipedia (http://en.wikipedia.org/wiki/Kaavya_Viswanathan) to glance at a comprehensive list of the passages she is said to have plagiarized.

Talking Points

1. List some ways in which the cases of Keller and Viswanathan are similar and different. If you wish, use the Venn diagram In Figure 1.1 as a guide for constructing your list.

2. While Viswanathan lost her reputation and book contract after she plagiarized, Keller's reputation has not suffered. Of the similarities and differences you listed, which do you think most affected the consequences each writer faced?

3. In your opinion, has each writer generally been treated fairly or unfairly? Do you tend to believe or disbelieve the explanations given by each girl?

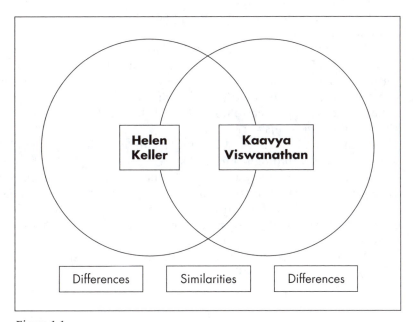

Figure 1.1

2 Copies (and Robberies)

How and Why Plagiarism Happens

"It's like our history class yesterday," Amanda says to me when I ask her class about cheating in our school. "We were in the library working on a quiz and the teacher walked out for a minute. We all immediately started talking about the answers even though she told us to be quiet before she left."

"You all cheated?" I ask.

"Well, sort of. But it was an open-book quiz, so we were all going to get the same answers anyway. She even took the questions straight out of the book."

Another student, Brittany, chimes in, "The questions were word for word from the book. We were just supposed to write down the next few sentences. It was dumb."

"Does that mean you plagiarized?" I ask.

"Maybe," Brittany answers. "I hadn't thought about it that way. But, uh, if we plagiarized, then so did the teacher, because she copied the exact words from the book, too. And anyway, we all knew the source. What, were we supposed to do an MLA [Modern Language Association] citation after every answer?"

Amanda adds, "That's the thing about our classes. We all know where the stuff's coming from. It's like when we copy stuff into a Power-Point, like you were talking about. I could always give you all the web pages, but who really cares? We're just going to trash it the next day."

"OK," I say. "But do you think that when you and a teacher copy straight from the book, that might make some students think it's OK to copy out of the book for other assignments?"

"Absolutely," Amanda says. "I think that happens all the time."

Brittany shrugs. "It's still no big deal."

YOU NEED TO KNOW: Understanding and Defining the Term *Plagiarism*

Many students think of *plagiarism* only as copying an entire essay and handing it in as one's own, when in fact the term refers to appropriating any material—ideas, writings, images, or portions of those—and claiming to be the original creator.

The word itself is interesting; its most immediate root is the Latin word *plagiarius*, meaning "kidnapper," but that word in turn comes from the older Latin word *plagus*, "net." The metaphors here might resonate with students. What does it mean to kidnap someone's ideas? How does the image of tossing a net over an object to capture it translate to capturing ideas from today's online Net?

It's also worth considering that plagiarism, which applies to questions of authorship, is slightly different from—though related to—forgery (which involves questions of authenticity), copyright infringement (which deals with legal ownership), and the broad label cheating (which implies purposeful deception of any type).

It may seem like splitting hairs to worry too much about definitions—we all know what it means to plagiarize, right? Perhaps teachers feel that they do, but parents, administrators, students, and the broader community may look for, and find, loopholes. Take the example of an eighth-grade teacher whose students turned in work copied verbatim from an encyclopedia, as is related in an excerpt from *Preventing Cheating and Plagiarism*:

> [The teacher] said they had plagiarized. Some of the kids' parents
> appealed to the school's Headmistress. Overruling the teacher, she
> decreed such copying was not plagiarism—at least not when done
> by 8th graders. (Clabaugh and Rozycki 2003)

It's worthwhile, therefore, to check whether your school or your teachers include a written definition of plagiarism in a school handbook or course syllabi. And if you have any doubts at all about the process you're using to complete your work, ask the teacher beforehand.

■ TALKING POINT

How would you respond to Amanda and Brittany? To what extent do you agree with Amanda that situations like the one she describes might help students rationalize plagiarism on other assignments? To what extent do you agree with Brittany that there are minor cases in which students don't follow the rules and that in those instances, it's "no big deal"?

Murky Waters: Plagiarism in Middle and High School

If you're anything like the students I teach, you've seen a lot of plagiarism, copying, and cheating while you've been in school. In fact, I can hear you now:

Of course I've seen a lot of cheating. Cheating goes on all the time. You think I don't know that?

Actually, I think you do know it. But I wonder how much you've really thought about plagiarism and what it means.

So you're saying if I read this book and think about cheating more, suddenly I won't want to cheat anymore?

I'm not that optimistic, but I do believe most students don't want to cheat—or plagiarize, in particular—just for the sake of cheating. I believe that the more you think about plagiarism and understand how and why you should avoid it, the more likely you are to do so.

But I don't plagiarize anyway! Why should I read this?

Of course *you* don't plagiarize. You're an angel.

Darn right I am.

But there are other reasons to keep reading. It's possible you've been *tempted* to plagiarize, and it's possible you'll run into difficult situations in the future, and it's even possible you've already plagiarized without realizing it and just didn't get caught. And it's possible, too, that you might know others who plagiarize on purpose or by accident and that you'll be the

Voices from the Classroom

I'm always afraid that I'll accidentally forget to cite something or have my quotation marks in the wrong place—not that any severe punishment will be exercised at my school, but that when I go to a college next year, it may not be seen as the mistake that it is because the teachers there won't know me yet and may put the honest me in a pool of those "cheating kids."

—*Laura, age seventeen*

Do you ever worry, like Laura, that an honest mistake might give your teachers the wrong impression of you? To what extent do you agree with Laura's expectations that the consequences of plagiarism in college may differ from those in middle or high school?

voice of reason. And there's more to this discussion than plagiarism—this is also a discussion about how and why you learn—but we have to start with the basics.

OK, fine, I'll keep reading.

See how easy that was? I'm glad we had this talk.

And are you really going to make up conversations with yourself? Because this could get a little creepy . . .

You've got a point there.

But then, so do I. The point is this: You might have heard conversations like the one that begins this chapter. Whether or not you agree with Amanda or Brittany, you can see that in some situations, the difference between cheating and not cheating is clear. In others, however, the waters get murky.

Most books and articles about plagiarism—as well as many teachers with whom I've spoken—assume that students plagiarize for one of two reasons: either they don't understand all of the rules (teachers call this unintentional plagiarism) or they're not sufficiently scared of what will happen if they get caught, so they copy from another source (intentional plagiarism). First of all, I think that it's not always quite so easy to distinguish intentional from unintentional plagiarism, and second of all, I think that even intentional plagiarism is often, though not always, more complicated than we give it credit for.

To begin, then, we need to distinguish types of plagiarism—*how* it happens—to make sure we're on the same page. Then we can talk about why plagiarism occurs and, finally, strategies for avoiding it.

> ### Voices from the Classroom
>
> Plagiarism? I'd define it as an easy A if you don't get caught, and an easy F if you do.
>
> —*Anton, age fourteen*
>
> Is Anton's definition accurate? Explain your response to his comment.

How Plagiarism Happens

Imagine that your best friend—let's call him, oh, Samuel Clemens—asks you to read his essay for English class:

> A father is suppose to wish the best for his children, but Pap seems to dislike the idea that his on is getting an education, becoming better that who he was. The new judge in town returns Huck to Pap because he privileges Pap's "rights" over Huck's welfare—just as slaves, because they were considered property, were regularly returned to their legal owners, no matter how badly these owners abused them. "You think you're better'n your father, now, don't you, because he can't?" These examples teach us something about Huck and about society. Huck is at

the center of countless failures and breakdowns in the society around him, yet he maintains his characteristic resilience.[1]

You read Sam's introductory paragraph, and then, knowing that he's about as likely to use a phrase like "characteristic resilience" as he is to write in Sumerian, you look back up at his innocent, blinking eyes. Did he plagiarize? The typos in the first sentence and the odd use of *privileges* as a verb seem realistic enough, but you're pretty certain good ole Sam hasn't even read the book. The question is: If he did plagiarize, how?

■ TALKING POINT

You know, if you read the footnote for Sam's paragraph, that it is plagiarized. We'll worry about *how* it was plagiarized in a moment. First, take a moment to discuss what you'd do if you were actually placed in the situation I described earlier. Would you confront your friend with your suspicions about his work? Would you ignore the possible plagiarism? Explain and discuss your answers with your classmates and teacher.

What's on the Menu? The Types of Plagiarism

Before we nail poor Sam for ripping off his opening paragraph, let me offer you a metaphor. It involves food, the Web, and plagiarism.

I love food, but sometimes even I have trouble sorting out what to eat and what to avoid at a potluck dinner. If you think about it, the Internet is a lot like one really big potluck. Nearly everyone in the world has brought a dish to the table. Some are delectable; others resemble the cornflake-topped eggplant casserole your wacky aunt used to produce at every family gathering; still others are practically poisonous or taste like school cafeteria food, no matter how lovely their appearance. The world of published words contains much nutritious and edible cuisine, but it can also be as hard to make a decision or to discern the ingredients in the library as it is with the online buffet table.

---

1. Confession time: While I received a paragraph similar to this one in class, I substituted the original offending paragraph with one I cobbled together myself from online sources. It contains plagiarized material that I *haven't* cited here just to make the point; all sources are identified and cited later in this chapter and are included in the Works Cited list at the end of the book.

My School, My Classroom

I asked nearly two hundred students in grades 7–12 at my school to tell me—anonymously—which types of plagiarism they had practiced within the last year. Students were allowed more than one answer. The answers, by percentage, appear in the chart below. While these results may not be an accurate reflection of national trends, they do paint an interesting picture of one group of suburban adolescents.

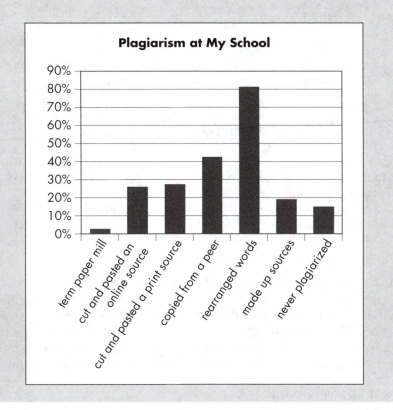

You need to eat, but you also need to eat wisely. You should know who made the dish and why. Know who uses only the freshest ingredients and who's likely to leave you with stomach cramps. Know the difference between taste and nutrition and make wise choices that give you both.

Our friend Sam may have indulged a bit too freely from the potluck choices. Let's consider the possibilities.

YOU NEED TO KNOW: How Widespread Is the Problem?

The following statistics represent the percentage of students who

- have engaged in cut-and-paste plagiarism: 40 percent (Muha 2003)

- say Internet plagiarism "is not a serious issue": 77 percent (Campbell 2007)

- have submitted a paper taken, in large part or in whole, from a term paper mill or website: 15 percent (iParadigms 2007)

- have copied a few sentences from a website without citing the source: 52 percent (iParadigms 2007)

- consider copying a few sentences without citation a "serious" offense: 35 percent (College Administration Publications n.d.)

Compare the results of these studies with your feelings about your own school. Would figures at your school be higher or lower? What does this say about the culture of your school and classes? Do you have any suggestions for change?

ORDERING IN: TERM PAPER MILLS AND CHEAT SITES

Perhaps Sam downloaded the entire paper—start to finish—from one of the hundreds of online sites that sell (or, sometimes, give away) papers, the ones with names like Schoolsucks.com and Itchybrainscentral.com. It's a scenario not that different from sticking an order of egg rolls from a Chinese restaurant onto a plate and claiming that you cooked them.

SURE, I COOKED THAT: PEER COPYING

If using a cheat site is the equivalent of ordering food from a restaurant and passing it off as your own creation, copying a friend's paper word for word is like switching the nameplates on the buffet table to take credit for what isn't yours. It happens fairly often—students are convinced teachers don't really read the papers (and sometimes, they might be correct) and therefore the assignment constitutes busywork, so why not take a shortcut? Of course, if Sam copied the *Huck Finn* essay from another student in the class, you might not catch it, but your teacher probably would.

THE SAMPLER PLATTER: CUTTING AND PASTING FROM MANY SOURCES

Students who cut and paste from the Internet cleverly don't just take several items from the buffet table; they then cobble them together into something that sounds original and resists detection. Did Sam's *Huck Finn* sentences come from several original sources?

ARTIFICIAL SWEETENER: THE POWER OF SUBSTITUTION

This approach is similar to ordering a pizza and, when it comes, throwing on toppings from your own refrigerator—and *then* claiming you cooked the whole thing. Maybe Sam copied sentences from the Internet and then replaced, say, every fifth word with a close synonym.

IS THIS FROM SCRATCH? THE PROBLEM WITH PARAPHRASING

Paraphrasing is, in fact, great reading practice. It's also a necessary and valuable skill for research writing; it helps you maintain a balance between quoting long passages of dreary material and failing to attribute your ideas. In fact, we'll revisit paraphrasing later in this chapter. If Sam thought he was paraphrasing another source, he did a poor job of it—there's no citation or acknowledgment of an original source anywhere in the paragraph, and therefore the work amounts to plagiarism of another's ideas.

MY MOM COOKED IT: TOO MUCH HELP FROM ANOTHER WRITER

Let's face it, sometimes your mom—or dad, or grandparent, or next door neighbor, or tutor—is just a better cook than you (or a better writer). There's no reason not to seek out advice and even some hands-on assistance from such a source, but there's also such a thing as too much help. Was that phrase about "characteristic resilience" in the sample paragraph written by Sam's older sister who's taking a college course in American literature, perhaps?

■ WRITE TO THE POINT

Take a look at Sam's paragraph again, and then, in the space below, describe the method you'd guess Sam used to plagiarize. Give two reasons for your suspicion—what in the paragraph leads you to think that Sam plagiarized in this particular way? Finally, explain how you'd go about trying to prove that Sam plagiarized. Be as specific as you can

(What web pages, books, or other sources might offer hard evidence of academic dishonesty?).

Type of Plagiarism	Two Reasons You Suspect This Type of Plagiarism	Where You'd Look for Proof
_____	1. _____	_____
_____	_____	_____
_____	_____	_____
_____	2. _____	_____
_____	_____	_____
_____	_____	_____

Learning Opportunities: Using the Menu to Your Advantage

Let's be clear: the point of asking you to think about types of plagiarism is *not* to make it possible for you to cheat more creatively. On the contrary, thinking about the menu of bad food allows you to seek out what's good for you with more certainty. In other words, you need to be sure that you are able to

- research online and printed material and cite it when necessary;
- paraphrase or summarize material from another source appropriately;
- find the correct format for in-text and bibliographic citations without difficulty;
- construct a system for note taking and research that works well for you;
- keep yourself from committing errors of judgment that result from pressure, confusion, carelessness, or apathy; and
- know how to get help on your writing without receiving too much help.

Your teachers can help you with some of these steps—determining citation format and creating strategies for studying and planning, for instance—but others are squarely your responsibility. We'll discuss these responsibilities and methods you might use to meet them throughout the rest of this book. Before moving on, however, let's deal with the nature of unintentional plagiarism and then with the areas of academic dishonesty

How Good Are Electronic Detection Services?

Remember the paragraph about *Huck Finn* at the start of this chapter? I tried checking it electronically myself in two ways:

1. *Google*. The good news: a quick Google search of the last sentence in the sample paragraph returned immediate results—the sentence was lifted directly out of the Spark-Notes chapter analysis for the novel (Martin and Martin n.d.). The bad news: having confirmed one example of plagiarism, I'm likely not to check the first, poorly written sentence. Read on.

2. *Turnitin.com*. Turnitin.com, in just a few seconds, accurately identified sentences 1, 2, 3, and 5 as plagiarized (yes, I composed sentence 4 myself). Take sentence 1, for instance, the poorly written line about Pap's view of Huck's education, which I would probably have assumed the student wrote. While Turnitin.com did not find the original source of the sentence (a pretty lousy paper from a term paper mill called 123helpme.com [n.d.]), it did make a 100 percent match to identical sentences in essays submitted by three other high school teachers around the country as well as to an earlier submission of the same paragraph I made myself. It also correctly identified, interestingly, the online text from which I lifted the precisely quoted material from the novel itself. Overall, a very useful report—and it took me, all told, about three minutes to submit the paper and review the results.

One must still be careful to study the report carefully—the site flags quoted as well as unquoted material. And, if you've posted your own work on the Internet, Turnitin.com might even catch that source and flag a paper for plagiarism because of it. Finally, a drawback of all electronic detection services and software is that work must be typed before it can be submitted. If you're dealing with large chunks of handwritten material you'd like to check to be sure you haven't plagiarized you're stuck either retyping the text or resorting to searching for a small piece at a time.

Note: The actual sources I used to create that paragraph are listed in the Works Cited section at the end of this book. They include a free student essay (sentence 1), the SparkNotes analysis (sentences 2 and 5), and an online version of the text from the University of Virginia Library (sentence 3; Cope 1995).

that are most often classified as unintentional plagiarism: paraphrasing, summarizing, and understanding the concept of common knowledge.

Good Intentions

We all know that in the real world your *intent* isn't always an excuse for breaking rules. You can try out a clever excuse ("I'm sorry, officer, but I thought it was legal to drive one hundred miles per hour because I have a sick dog at home who needs me—really!"), but it doesn't always help.

Earlier, I mentioned that teachers often divide plagiarism into intentional and unintentional cases. That doesn't mean that ignorance is an excuse, but it does help you see how some of the types of plagiarism I described earlier might occur. Some acts of plagiarism are deliberate while others almost certainly occur by accident, but many fall into a gray area in between, and knowing they exist can help you avoid mistakes you'll regret later. Take a look at Figure 2.1 and consider the acts that might fall into the gray area between intentional and unintentional plagiarism I've described.

■ TALKING POINTS

1. Is it possible that the same act might be a case of intentional plagiarism in one situation and unintentional plagiarism in another? What about, say, copying material directly out of a textbook for an assignment? Discuss any moments from your own experience in which teachers have sent the message that such practices are—or are not—acceptable.

2. Just because an action falls higher or lower on the circle in Figure 2.1, do you think it deserves a harsher punishment? What other factors might influence a decision about the consequences a student should face in response to an act of plagiarism?

Learning Opportunities: *Make It Black and White*

As I said, some decisions fall into a gray area between absolutely intentional and unintentional plagiarism, and you may often feel caught in a difficult situation. How, for instance, would you respond to the following scenarios (all of which were suggested by real students)?

- Your English teacher tells your class it would be a good idea for you to work with a partner on your vocabulary homework. After

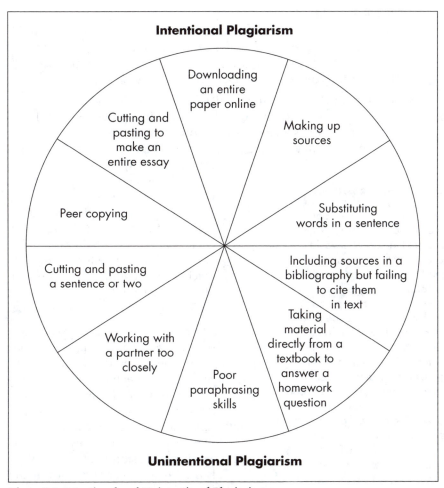

Intentional Plagiarism

Downloading an entire paper online

Cutting and pasting to make an entire essay

Making up sources

Peer copying

Substituting words in a sentence

Cutting and pasting a sentence or two

Including sources in a bibliography but failing to cite them in text

Working with a partner too closely

Taking material directly from a textbook to answer a homework question

Poor paraphrasing skills

Unintentional Plagiarism

Figure 2.1 Intentional and Unintentional Plagiarism

school, a friend suggests that this means the two of you should divide of words in half, find definitions and sample sentences on your own, and then copy the other half of the list from each other. Do you agree? Why or why not?

- In a history class, you are expected to include ten citations in a paper. The rubric states that each error in a citation will lower the grade by five points, and that any paper with no citations at all will automatically receive thirty points off. Your friend, who frequently makes numerous errors on such assignments, decides to leave out all of the citations in her paper (even though she used some outside sources) and accept the 70 percent, since she could potentially lose even more points for making too many errors. Is your friend making a smart move, or should she complete all of the citations despite the greater risk to her grade?

- During lunch, you describe an art history project you've been assigned to a student who took the class in a previous year. The student describes a clever way of organizing and presenting the information that he used on the same assignment and promises that if you copy his overall format—though you'll still have to write out descriptions on your own—you'll get a high grade. If you take his advice, will you be cheating or fairly collaborating? Do you feel responsible for telling the teacher where your organizational ideas come from?

One thing is certain: in any scenario I could provide that illustrates potential plagiarism, it would be better if the student consulted with the teacher *before* completing the assignment. You may have heard the old adage that suggests it's easier to ask forgiveness than permission, but in cases of possible academic dishonesty, it's far better to seek permission first.

It also helps to know the rules in the first place. Simply put, you won't commit plagiarism by accident if you make accidents impossible, and the way to do that is know what you're doing.

You already know that when you quote information you must identify the source. You probably also know *how* to cite a source, and if you don't, I'm sure your teachers can provide you with examples. The rest of this chapter deals with two areas in which you should know (and might not) the generally accepted rules of scholarship: paraphrasing and summariz-

---

Voices from the Classroom

Plagiarism comes hand in hand with procrastination and laziness. In our school, plagiarism occurs more than anyone would like, but I will have to admit the majority of the students are much more clever about it than your everyday "print an essay offline and hand it in" scenario. Paraphrasing and the copy-and-paste function become the instant companion to any student wishing to get an assignment done, just to attain the goal of turning it in on time with minimum effort.

My general opinion is that plagiarism is something too idiotic to risk getting caught and being deemed an "immoral" student. I used to be one of the over-achievers who got by sometimes with easy As by cheating or copying work. I learned the hard way that this not only has large consequences on the teacher-student-parent trust level, but also for someone who spends so much time avoiding doing work, in the end nothing good comes to you in return. I am happy to say I do my own work now, and as an end result have improved my writing and work ethics immensely.

—*Beverly, age eighteen*

Beverly says that she changed but doesn't explain why she changed, other than that she "learned the hard way." What do think she means by that? What might "the hard way" entail other than direct punishments from teachers or administrators?

ing, followed by the concept of common knowledge.

Boiling It Down: Rules for Paraphrasing and Summarizing

Recently, a ninth-grade student turned in the following two sentences for a six-page honors-level biology report assigned by a teacher I know:

> Sickle-cell anemia, a blood disorder caused when red blood cells assume an abnormal shape like a sickle, is caused by cells that don't last as long as round cells and are deprived of oxygen. The painful disease causes organ damage, period attacks, and is chronic.

Yes, I know, what's painful here is not just the disease but the assignment. Welcome to ninth-grade biology.

When the student's teacher typed "sickle-cell anemia" into a search engine, he immediately retrieved the following passages. Note that the student's writing does not *quite* summarize either passage accurately.

> ### Voices from the Classroom
>
> When I write papers in which outside sources are used, I usually just copy and paste the URL and go back to the site later when I am ready to write the bibliography. Some sites, however, allow people to see it for a limited time, but after that they have to have a password and agree to all this stuff to see it again. This occurred with me a couple of months ago. I was typing up the bibliography and I clicked on the URL I had pasted in my paper. The window came up saying that this site was blocked. The quote I had received from the site, however, was really good and fit perfectly for my paper. So, I changed the internal citations, and said they were from a different document.
>
> *—Janice, age seventeen*
>
> If you were to find, as Janice did, a useful quotation but couldn't track down the source, would you still use it?

Internet Sample 1

Sickle-cell disease is a blood disorder characterised by red blood cells that assume an abnormal, rigid, sickle shape. Sickling decreases the cells' flexibility and results in their restricted movement through blood vessels, depriving downstream tissues of oxygen. The disease is chronic and lifelong: individuals are most often well, but their lives are punctuated by periodic painful attacks. (Wikipedia contributors 2008)

Internet Sample 2

Sickle cell anemia is a disease in which your body produces abnormally shaped red blood cells. The cells are shaped like a crescent or sickle. They don't last as long as normal, round red blood cells, which leads to anemia. The sickle cells also get stuck in blood vessels, blocking blood flow. This can cause pain and organ damage. (U.S. National Library of Medicine 2008)

■ WRITE TO THE POINT

The student who summarized the information from these two sources made several errors. Describe at least two ways in which this student could have improved his paragraph.

_____

_____

_____

_____

_____

_____

_____

The problem with paraphrasing, frankly, is that most students haven't learned to do it well. Paraphrasing is a legitimate practice so long as credit is given. The Harvard University guide for students called *Writing with Internet Sources*, for instance, warns students of the dangers of excessive paraphrasing, paraphrasing without citation, rewording material too closely, and failing to keep notes of material that might come up in a written assignment (Burg et al. 2007). And, just to make the point, I paraphrased the guide in my previous sentence instead of quoting it.

Figure 2.2 offers three versions of the same material, taken from a chapter on writing research papers in *The Bedford Introduction to Literature* (Meyer 1993). Take a look, especially, at the *incorrect* paraphrase and you'll see how easy it is to slightly reword a passage without attribution or quotation. (All classroom examples and assignments are cited according to MLA rules.)

Practice Makes Perfect (Even if It's a Bother)

Paraphrasing is, in fact, great reading practice. It's also a necessary and valuable skill for research writing; it helps students maintain a balance between quoting long passages of dreary material and failing to attribute their ideas.

Original Source	Incorrect Paraphrase	Correct Paraphrase
"Some mention should be made of the notion of common knowledge before we turn to the standard format for documenting sources. Observations and facts that are widely known and routinely included in many of your sources do not require documentation. It is not necessary to cite a source for the fact that Alfred, Lord Tennyson was born in 1809 or that Ernest Hemingway loved to fish and hunt." (Meyer 2076)	It's worth noting that in a research paper, common knowledge need not be documented. Data that is universally learned, like the date of Tennyson's birth or Hemingway's love of hunting, is exempt from the need for documentation.	According to Meyer, facts and observations that are widely known, such as Tennyson's birth or Hemingway's love of hunting, constitute a body of common knowledge that does not require documentation (2076).

Figure 2.2

Figure 2.3 is a short worksheet intended to help you focus on three aspects of incorporating another text into one's own work:

- First, the exercise encourages you to consider the difference between paraphrasing and plagiarizing by not just rewording but also restating the passage.
- Next, the exercise guides you in quoting and attributing ideas from the original passage.
- Finally, the exercise guides you toward the most important aspect of paraphrasing—the skill of using a paraphrase in conjunction with your own ideas about a topic to produce a new, original piece of writing.

Try this worksheet, and if you have any questions, discuss them with your teacher or classmates.

Paraphrasing Practice

Important Terms

Plagiarizing: copying words or ideas that aren't your own without citing the source

Allusion: a reference to another story or character

Paraphrasing: restating an idea in your own words

Citing: noting in the text (usually by putting the author's name in parentheses) the source of an idea or quotation

First, read the passage below:

Plagiarism seeks to conceal the source, while allusion seeks to reveal it. In creative writing (poetry, fiction, drama, memoir), you may indeed include allusions. These are references to other texts that extend your meaning. But in academic writing (essays, research, argumentation, lab reports), you must document all of your sources. ("Academic Integrity")

Now, answer these questions:

1. According to the paragraph, what is the difference between plagiarism and allusion?

_____

_____

_____

2. Find the most important sentence and write it below.

_____

_____

_____

_____

3. Circle the most important three or four words in that sentence and write them below.

_____

4. Paraphrase the sentence you identified in question 2. You may use two words from your answer to question 3 *but no other words from the original sentence.*

_____

_____

_____

_____

Figure 2.3

Paraphrasing Practice, continued

Citation Reminders

- For MLA format, put the author's name and page number in parentheses: (Smith 92).

- Place the period after the parentheses (see above). There is no comma between the name and page number.

- If you use the author's name in the sentence, you don't have to include it at the end.

- If you access the source online, no page number is needed.

- Remember to place the source in your bibliography, as well.

5. Write a sentence of your own in which you quote from the paragraph. Use quotation marks and a citation at the end of the sentence.

_____

_____

_____

6. In the space below, describe one instance in which the author of the paragraph might be *wrong*. When might you use an allusion in academic writing?

_____

_____

_____

_____

7. Now write a paragraph of your own. In your writing, comment on the original paragraph—do you mostly agree or mostly disagree? At some point in your answer, either quote the original paragraph and cite it or paraphrase the original paragraph and cite it.

_____

_____

_____

_____

_____

_____

_____

Works Cited

Grace Hauenstein Library. n.d. "Academic Integrity." Aquinas College. www.aquinas.edu/library/plagiarism.html (accessed Feb. 18, 2008).

Figure 2.3

Remember that there are rules for paraphrasing, summarizing, and quoting. Your teachers have probably introduced you to the idea that quotations should be blended into papers smoothly and following certain guidelines, such as using block quotation format for longer passages. A discussion of the mechanics of quoting is valuable, and knowing the rules will help you avoid plagiarism. For our purposes, what's more important is understanding the distinctions between quotation, plagiarism, and summary and being true to the spirit of scholarship and ongoing dialogue these tools make possible.

So here's a handy guide. Figure 2.4 may help you remember when to use each of the tools of information gathering and the most important aspects of using them without plagiarizing.

Aye, Madam, 'Tis Common: The Spirit of Common Knowledge and Citation

If you're anything like the students I've taught for the past fifteen years, you're asking some questions in your head by now. (Warning: here comes another one of those crazy pseudoconversations. Sorry, but it turns out you have more to say.)

So you're telling me I have to change every *word or else quote it. What about words like* the? *Or* a? *Where does it all end?*

Once again, you have a point.

Thanks.

You're welcome. Look, no one's telling you to put quotation marks around "*the*" (even though I just did). And if you're writing a paper about, oh, albino peacocks, no one's going to argue if you say you couldn't find too many synonyms for *peacock*—or *albino*—to substitute in your paraphrase. But once you describe anything about those peacocks, unless you happen to be an expert on the subject because you raise the things as a hobby, you'll need to either find your own words or put quotation marks around the fact that albino peacocks are extremely rare or that they love to ride in canoes.

Hey, you made up that thing about canoes, right?

Yes, I did.

It's true: There are a few cases in which you don't need to cite material. These cases are called "common knowledge" and they include widely known, factual information such as dates (Shakespeare died in 1616) or statistics (Shakespeare wrote 154 sonnets). The quick litmus test for such knowledge is whether you can find it easily in at least three sources, but most of the time you can recognize common knowledge without actually looking it up—that's the point of calling it common. If you're the least bit concerned, cite the source. If you have any doubt

	Quotation	Paraphrase	Summary
Use this tool . . .	to include words or phrases originally written by another author	to avoid including an overly long quotation in your work	to recount a single main idea from another (usually much longer) source
	Example "Knowing the rules will help you avoid plagiarism" insists one author (Gilmore 24).	**Example** Gilmore, for instance, suggests that a knowledge of the rules, while important, may be less so than understanding the spirit of scholarship (24).	**Example** Throughout his writing, Gilmore again and again draws a distinction between knowing rules and understanding why they exist.
And also . . .	when you wish to emphasize the language or phrasing of an original source	to condense and explain technical or complicated material from another source	when the overall information is important but the details are not
	Example Gilmore compares the Internet to an "online buffet table" (10), suggesting through his metaphor that too many students don't care about the nutritional value of what they find there.	**Example** Methods of plagiarism may range from wholesale downloading of essays from term paper mills (Internet sites that provide such papers to students) to cut-and-paste techniques that involve copying chunks of text from other sources and passing them off as one's own (Gilmore 12–13).	**Example** Gilmore's discussion of plagiarism techniques common to students leads us to consider more important questions about how and why students learn.
Before you write . . .	include quotations in their original context; be true to the author's original meaning	be accurate; don't distort any ideas from the original source	be accurate; don't distort any ideas from the original source
	REALLY BAD Examples (Don't do this!) Gilmore believes that students should eat wisely while they study, thus eliminating plagiarism by avoiding visits to the "buffet table" (10).	**REALLY BAD Examples (Don't do this!)** Gilmore lists term paper mills such as Itchybrainscentral.com in order to help students cheat more easily (12).	**REALLY BAD Examples (Don't do this!)** According to Gilmore, students should avoid the dangers of the Internet and its poisonous offerings at all costs.

Figure 2.4

	Quotation	**Paraphrase**	**Summary**
When you write . . .	do not change any text—not even a single word—from the original source unless you denote that text by including it in brackets **Example** Gilmore suggests that students adhere to the "spirit of scholarship" as well as the specific rules (24).	use your own phrasing as much as possible; while it may be impossible to avoid repeating some words, don't use any *consecutive* words without placing them in quotation marks, and use synonyms wherever you can **Example** Gilmore suggests that while rules exist, the reasons those rules exist may be more important for students to understand (24).	use your own phrasing as much as possible; place any words from the original source in quotation marks **Example** Throughout his writing, Gilmore again and again draws a distinction between knowing rules and understanding the "spirit of scholarship" (24).
After you write . . .	cite your source in your sentence following the quote **Example** The comparison of some websites to the "corn-flake-topped eggplant casserole" one might find served at a family dinner points out the need to use reputable web sources (Gilmore 10).	cite your source after your restatement of ideas **Example** Gilmore outlines six methods of plagiarism: downloading, peer copying, cutting and pasting, intentionally substituting words, paraphrasing poorly, and having parents or others complete assignments (12–13).	cite your source after your summary **Example** At least six methods of plagiarism are commonly used by students in today's schools (Gilmore).
Check to be sure that . . .	quotations are included in (or, for block quotations, introduced by) a grammatical sentence of your own in which you provide context for the author's words, establish a relationship to your ideas, and include any information necessary for understanding the quotation (such as a description of irony or humor)	you've given clues to the reader so that he can tell when you begin and finish paraphrasing	you've given clues to the reader when you begin and finish the summary, especially if you use more than one sentence to summarize

Figure 2.4

	Quotation	**Paraphrase**	**Summary**
Check to be sure that . . .	**Example** The comparison of some web sites to the "corn-flake-topped eggplant casserole" (Gilmore 10) one might find served at a family dinner points out the need to use reputable web sources.	**Example** Gilmore outlines six methods of plagiarism: downloading, peer copying, cutting and pasting, intentionally substituting words, paraphrasing poorly, and having parents or others complete assignments (12–13). The last of these merits special attention here...	**Example** Is there more than one way to cheat? One author suggests that at least six methods of plagiarism are commonly used by students in today's schools (Gilmore). Yet Gilmore's list may not be comprehensive...

Figure 2.4

about the truth of the statement (Shakespeare wrote his sonnets to an albino peacock), look it up, then cite the source.

The bottom line is this: You owe it to other people to give them credit where it's due. The law provides for fair use of small pieces of others' work (there's no absolute word or page limit, but the key word is *small*), but that law doesn't release you from the responsibility of crediting others for ideas, words, images, music, or any other intellectual property. Most of the time, common sense will tell you when a source is offering a widely known fact about peacocks or an expert opinion about them. It will help you realize that the title of this section (it's an allusion to *Hamlet*) doesn't need citation, but that a quotation in your analytical paper does (because your readers might want to go and find it). And that same common sense will keep you from quoting the word *the* and help you put quotation marks around phrases that need them because, after all, they belong to someone else.

So we've come to the end of the beginning: how students plagiarize, mistakes they make that lead to plagiarism, and how you can avoid those mistakes. What's left, you ask? Oh, there's more. Coming up: why you should avoid plagiarism (there may be more to that conversation than you expect) and the bigger questions, such as where the road to plagiarism begins and how to avoid starting down that path.

But for now, remember that you own the knowledge you need to avoid most types of plagiarism and cheating; there are no excuses.

■ CASE STUDY: TAKE IT OR LEAVE IT

One of the most famous recent cases of battling Internet plagiarism at the high school level involves a teacher named Christine Pelton, who turned to Turnitin.com when she suspected widespread plagiarism in response to a major assignment in her biology class. The project in question was called the Leaf Project: students had to classify and write information about a number of different kinds of leaves, then present their findings to the class. The assignment counted for 50 percent of the first-semester grade.

Almost one-quarter of her sophomores, it turned out, had plagiarized material from the Internet.

What was really interesting about this case was that Pelton had students *and* parents sign a contract that included a plagiarism rule at the start of the year. Yet after she failed the students, parents appealed to the school board, who overruled Pelton and her immediate supervisor, the school principal. The board reduced the value of the assignment to 30 percent of the semester grade and thus allowed students who would have failed the course to pass.

The parents' contention, in part, was that their children hadn't been taught how *not* to plagiarize. One student spoke anonymously to the CBS show *48 Hours* about the situation:

> "I was kind of upset 'cause I was pretty sure I did't do it," he says, claiming he copied from the internet but didn't plagiarize. . . . "I put that as two different sentences," he says. "So it's not like I copied it straight from the Web site. I changed it into two different sentences." (2002)

Pelton resigned over the situation immediately; other teachers resigned at the end of the school year.

Find Out More

Try conducting a quick web search for "Christine Pelton"—I came up with around seventy-five thousand hits. Read a few of the articles you find, or go to the Works Cited section of this book to find the report from *48 Hours* quoted earlier. As you read the articles, look for any other information that might influence your feelings about the case (and remember to keep track of your sources!).

Talking Points

1. Do you believe the student quoted in the *48 Hours* interview plagiarized intentionally or unintentionally? What evidence from the student's words supports your position?

2. No article I could find questioned the merit of the Leaf Project or described the specific elements or use of class time it included. Would any information in this area have the potential to change your feelings about the case? Why do you think this information is not broadly reported?

3. Overall, do you tend to agree most with Pelton, the students and their parents, or the school board? Explain your answer.

4. How would you feel about the case if you were one of the students who plagiarized? How would you feel about it if you hadn't plagiarized and made an A on the original assignment? What would the consequences be in each case?

5. If you were a teacher in Pelton's school, would you be tempted to resign over this case?

3 *Write from Wrong*

Why You Should Avoid Plagiarism

To begin this part of our discussion, take this pop quiz:

1. (Circle all that apply.) Within the last year, I have:
    a. downloaded a song from the Internet without paying the artist
    b. watched a movie or television show online without paying for it
    c. copied an image from the Internet and used it without citing the source
    d. borrowed a recording (CD, etc.) from a friend and made a copy of it for myself

2. (Answer only if you circled at least one answer above.) When I committed this offense, I felt:
    a. guilty
    b. not guilty

Now read on.

The Ethics Gap

It's probably no secret to you that your teachers think differently than you do. Yes, this may be because some sort of swampy alien beings have secretly been assuming human form with a covert master plan of making the world's youth miserable and taking over the planet. Some of the students I teach certainly think this is the case.

The more likely explanation is that times change between one generation and the next; the context of learning in the twenty-first century is not the same as it was in the twentieth century (or the nineteenth, or whatever century it was when that ancient math teacher down the hall was born).

Why does this matter? Believe it or not, most teachers *try* to keep up with the changes in technology, culture, and viewpoint that have shifted the educational landscape, as well. Your teachers may not download music online or visit Facebook or watch videos on YouTube, but they're probably familiar with how and why students use the Internet in these ways. But no matter how hard they try, there may still exist what I call an ethics gap between students and teachers in your school.

This ethics gap may manifest in different ways. Think, for instance, about the list on pages 32–33.

The Web of Culture and the Culture of the Web

As a student of the Wikipedia era, you may well have circled one or more of the items on the pop quiz that begins this chapter and also have circled "not guilty" on the second question. If you didn't, you probably know people who would. Students who regularly download material from the Internet, who believe that because the material is free it can't be protected by law, or who have just grown up pooling information online (Wikipedia's a good example of this) may have a completely different view of what constitutes appropriate use than their teachers do.

Add to this the complicated nature of downloading. As I wrote this, you could watch four seasons of the hit television show *Lost* on the site of a major network without paying a dime—and without breaking any laws. You could watch any season of *American Idol* online, too, but to do so you had to visit a site that posts the episodes in violation of copyright laws. Why is one OK but not the other? Add to *that* the fact that *you* personally probably won't face any direct consequences no matter what shows you watch (though the sites that post copyrighted material may face serious consequences, and you shouldn't take a probable lack of consequences as permission to break the law). And add to *that* the fact that if the networks change their minds, tomorrow *Lost* could be unavailable to you just as *American Idol* becomes fair game.

It doesn't always seem to make sense. Still, there are rules. Take the words you're reading right now. For better or worse, boring or not, as soon as I wrote them in a particular order, they belonged to me. If my publisher and I wanted to give them away, we could, and if we wanted to sell them, we could do that, too. That was our choice to make—not yours, not your teacher's, or some other guy's who thinks they'd be great on his web page. You can quote these words (I know, I know—why the heck would you want to?), but you can't suddenly copy the whole book for your cheapskate cousin in Omaha (no offense to people from Omaha—nice place) so that she doesn't have to pay for it. In other words, there are rules.

TOP TEN: Reasons Students Give for Plagiarizing

1. Confusion about the procedure:

   "I don't know what all those terms mean—*citation, attribution, quotation*—what's the difference?"

   "I thought I didn't need to cite facts."

   "I didn't think I needed to cite for minor assignments."

   "I couldn't find the source again after I put it in my notes—I didn't think it mattered."

2. Procrastination:

   "The deadline crept up on me."

3. Pressure:

   "My parents want me to make good grades."

   "If I don't make a good grade, I'll lose my privileges."

4. Avoidance:

   "I thought I could get away with it."

   "I didn't want to do the assignment."

5. Confusion about the assignment:

   "I didn't understand the directions."

   "I didn't want to use too many sources."

   "I thought we were *supposed* to copy the answers from the book."

6. Student culture:

   "In my culture, it's considered flattering to use someone else's words."

   "We just don't cite that way in schools in my country."

   "My English language skills aren't good enough to understand the sources."

7. School culture:

   "Everyone else does it—why should I suffer for being honest?"

   "Teachers don't really care—in fact, they encourage it."

   "It's no big deal—that's the way the system works."

8. Self-doubt:

   "I'm no good at writing."

   "I'll never get it right, anyway."

9. Disdain for the assignment:

   "When will I ever need to know this stuff?"

   "The content doesn't matter—I'm just here for the grade."

   "This is just busywork."

10. Collaboration:

    "I thought we could work together."

Believe me, it's not like I'm so rich from writing about plagiarism that your money's going to pay for a private yacht with a butler named Jeeves carrying cheese puffs around on a silver dish, but I'm not the only one earning money from this book. The proofreaders and editors and cover artists and a bunch of people earn from it, too, just as the folks who work on the set of *American Idol* earn their money (you can ask them about that, I suppose, if you can catch up to *their* yachts).

The point, of course, is not about my book or my money. It's about the fact that when you plagiarize, you steal—yes, and sometimes you actually steal money as well as ideas, though both are bad—from real people, just as you do when you download a song or movie from an illegal site.

The point is also that your teachers grew up in a world in which copyright issues were pretty obvious. You can photocopy a poem for a class of students, for instance, but you can't photocopy an entire novel. But the Internet has blurred many of those lines, and even where the lines are fixed, many of us don't know what those lines look like.

■ TALKING POINTS

1. Back to the quiz: Do you agree with me when I assert that watching a movie online illegally or copying an image without attribution is similar to plagiarizing in a student essay? If not, what distinctions would you make between these acts?

2. Do you think an ethics gap exists in your school? What do the opposing sides of this gap look like? What do you or other students believe that your teachers or administrators see differently? Are there any other groups who view appropriate use of online materials differently than you do and, if so, who?

The Rules of Victory

I first heard the phrase "the rules of victory" in the context of plagiarism from a colleague who teaches at the college level. He explained it by relating what he tells students on the first day of class.

"My purpose," my friend tells his classes, "is to get you to read, to think, to learn, to reflect. Your purpose may be to get a decent grade, whatever that takes. Some days I'll win. Some days you'll win. At the end of the course, what you take away and what I take away from the experience both depend on our rules for victory."

Looked at in this way, a plagiarized paper isn't so different from an original paper that avoids any risks, depth of thought, or original analysis. The former avoids learning to achieve a grade; so does the latter. One may break the rules and the other follow them, but the end result is, in the most practical terms, the same.

It sounds like a simple question, but it gets to the heart of how you learn: What are your rules for victory? What do you walk into a class thinking you'll take away? How does that attitude compare with the attitude of your teachers? Your parents? Your friends?

■ WRITE TO THE POINT

In the space below, describe your rules for victory. When you walked into your current class, what did you hope to get out of it? Make a list of your expectations for the class or just generally describe them, then consider how those expectations might differ from the rules for victory of other students, your teacher, or your parents.

_____

_____

_____

_____

_____

Recognizing that an ethics gap exists is a first step, and figuring out how the people on either side of that gap feel about learning is a second. And keep in mind: Your teachers don't all think the same, either. Take, for instance, rules about collaboration. Your science teacher may want you to borrow notes from a friend and your history teacher might consider that cheating. I talked to one former student (he didn't want to be named) who was brought up on charges of plagiarism by a college professor after he went to the *college's* writing center for proofreading help on an essay.

You've got to know the rules, but not only the ones set in stone by the MLA or the American Psychological Association (APA) or some other disembodied, acronymed organization. You've also got to know the rules teachers set for their own classrooms, whether those rules are explicit or implicit, and the only way to find out is to talk to your teachers. If you're reading this book with a class, you could stop right now and ask your teacher for a list of rules, but no matter how hard that teacher tries, unforeseen situations will arise. It's better to ask before each assignment, when you're thinking about how you'll work on a project. As I said before, the old adage that it's easier to ask forgiveness than permission is not true about plagiarism—forgiveness is hard, while permission clarifies. If there's an ethics gap, build a bridge across it, meet in the middle, whatever it takes, but don't just stand on your side waving like an idiot and pretending you won't be the one to plunge headfirst into the abyss if it comes down to that.

YOU NEED TO KNOW: Memory Lapse, or Lapse in Judgment?

Plagiarists throughout history have claimed innocence by maintaining that they didn't recall actually getting material from another source. Is there truly such a thing as unconscious plagiarism? According to recent studies reported in *The Boston Globe*, the phenomenon—called *cryptomnesia* by experts—may be more common than we think, occurring in 8 to 12 percent of subjects in one test and up to 20 percent in others (Goldberg 2006).

One interesting line of thought arising from such tests is summed up by researcher Richard Marsh in the same article: "when people are busy trying to be creative, they tend to fail to consider where their ideas come from and can inadvertently steal." Learning to combat such tendencies is partly a matter of training— copying down a URL or book title in one's notes beside a summary of material without slowing down the creative process, then formatting a full bibliographical entry later on, for instance. The idea of such inadvertent theft ought also, however, to warn us against assuming that every plagiarized word is a malicious crime.

The Bottom Line: Paying the Consequences

Plagiarism's embarrassing. It's not just picking-your-nose-in-public embarrassing, either; plagiarism makes an announcement to the world. You may wish that this announcement included the immense pressures you're under, your confusion about process, or your momentary errors in judgment, but the message people usually read into an act of plagiarism is something more along the lines of *Hey, I didn't want to do this and I was too much of a nitwit not to cheat* and *get caught cheating.*

If you were to make a list of reasons *why* you shouldn't plagiarize, they'd probably all fall into one of three categories:

1. It's not fair to others to take their ideas without credit.

2. It's not fair to yourself not to learn from original writing and thinking.

3. There are direct consequences—short-term and long-term—if you get caught.

It's tough, I've found, to sell middle and high school students—and even college students or adults—on reasons 1 and 2 unless they've somehow internalized the lesson. I can tell you it's wrong, but it doesn't matter unless you feel and believe it's wrong, and those lessons will come mostly from your own experience. Similarly, I can get you to think about your own learning, but that learning is ultimately yours to control.

My School, My Classroom

My survey of around two hundred students, grades 7–12, in my own school produced data for the following two charts. The first chart shows the responses of these students to the question, "Why do you think most students at our school plagiarize?" Notice how little credence these students give to the notion that confusion or school culture encourage academic dishonesty (though it is important to note that student perception of motivations is not necessarily accurate). The second chart shows the responses of the students to the question, "How serious an offense do you think it is to copy a homework assignment or essay from a peer?" Interestingly, while only a few students classified this act as "not serious at all," only a few considered it to be "very serious," with the vast majority falling somewhere in the middle.

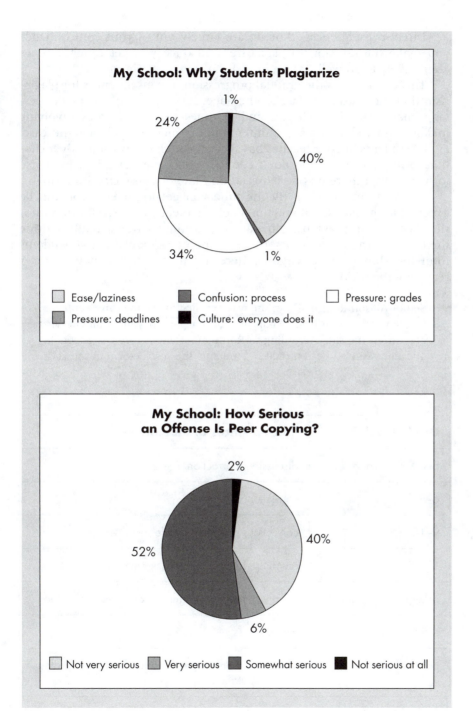

Direct consequences, though, are largely out of your control. Once you make the decision to plagiarize, and once you get caught, things aren't likely to go well. Take a look, for instance, at Figure 3.1.

This chart shows the gradual progression of consequences for plagiarism that most students face as they age. It's not exact; this model pertains mainly to first offenses and assumes that most cases involving middle school students are unintentional, which isn't always the case. For all students, if your teacher has spent three class days going over citation format and then you don't cite, the consequences might be worse for you than if there was no expectation that you'd use citation format.

But you get the idea. By the time you get to college, you can be expelled for plagiarism. If you don't believe me, do a search for news stories. Within the previous four days of the time I was actually writing these words, there was a major case in the news involving two students from the University of Virginia. Here are pieces of two news articles reporting the incident:

> Senior Allison Routman says she was expelled for taking three sentence fragments verbatim from Wikipedia and for paraphrasing a movie synopsis from the site. According to Routman, a day before the papers in question were to be returned to students, the instructor told the class

Grade Level	Consequences of Plagiarism
below 6th grade	discussion, correction
6–8	correction, rewriting
9–10	correction, rewriting, grade penalties
11–12	rewriting, failure on the assignment
college undergraduate	rewriting, failure (assignment or course), expulsion
graduate student	expulsion
professional	loss of job/contract, legal penalties, loss of professional reputation

Figure 3.1

plagiarism was suspected and asked students to come forward and make a "conscientious retraction." Routman says she did not think she had done anything wrong at the time, so she did not come forward. "Had I had any idea I had done something wrong, I would have absolutely come forward," she said. . . . She was later confronted and expelled. The appeal she mounted was also dismissed. (Go 2008)

Routman said her class assignment was to watch a movie, then write a paper relating the film to shipboard or port experiences. She watched "Europa Europa" and consulted Wikipedia for the proper historic terminology. The professor alleged that she used three phrases identical to those on the online entry about the movie: "when the Germans attacked the Soviet Union during Operation Barbarossa," "German speaking minority outside of Germany" and "who had been released from a concentration camp." (Sampson 2008)

■ TALKING POINTS

1. With whom do you most agree in this situation, the professor or Routman?

2. If you were a teacher and found an exact phrase from a student's paper online by googling it, what assumptions might you make about the rest of the paper or the rest of that student's work?

Whether you agree with the professor, the university, or the student, Routman, this example shows you the consequences of carelessness. It shows that ignorance doesn't always get you off the hook. It shows you that plagiarism is trouble.

That's not to say that many teachers aren't more sympathetic than the professor in the example. We know that students are under a great deal of pressure, more even than they sometimes realize themselves. Take a look at Figure 3.2 to see what I'm talking about—as you look at this chart, ask yourself how many of the pressures pushing on the student in the center you also feel on a regular basis.

Some teachers, in fact, feel so much empathy for students under pressure that they don't report cases of plagiarism at all. I'm not against second chances, and I even encourage teachers to give them (I also encourage schools to use systems in which they record first instances of plagiarism without enforcing severe punishments so that second instances don't slip by unnoticed).

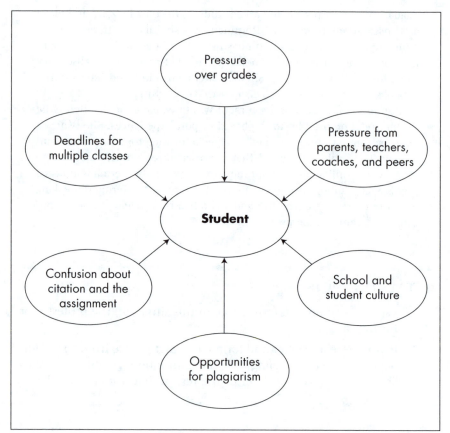

Figure 3.2

Yet, as I've said before, the responsibility for avoiding plagiarism is yours, not your teacher's or your school's. Teachers and schools can sometimes make accommodations that relieve the pressures students feel, and they should do so when they can, but pressure doesn't excuse academic dishonesty, does it? So what's the best thing? Avoid the pressures when you can reasonably do so, and when you can't, try to see them coming in advance so that you can deal with them through time management, discussion with teachers or parents, and good planning. That's up to you. Fail to take that kind of responsibility, and you may find yourself *wishing* you'd picked your nose in public instead of plagiarizing and having to face the consequences that come with that choice.

Mother Knows Best (but She Still Shouldn't Write Your Papers for You)

A few years ago, I sat in a parent conference and listened as a student's mother proudly explained to me the process she and her son used to complete his essays. First he would make an outline and collect the evidence, then they would discuss it together, then he would write a rough draft, and then she would type the draft for him.

"When you type the paper," I asked, "do you make corrections for him?"

"I don't change anything major," she said. "I just correct spelling and syntax and grammar."

A little more probing revealed that the mother, a college professor, had designed for her son a sentence-by-sentence template for his essays. I recognized that communication was going to be an ongoing issue in this case. I also recognized, however, that this mother was one who cared deeply about her son's education, who wanted him to learn and do well in school, who was willing to talk with me openly and frankly about her involvement, and who was, in many ways, working against all that I was trying to accomplish in the classroom, albeit unintentionally.

Had I used the word *plagiarism* to describe her son's papers, I have no doubt that the conference would have taken a wildly different turn—I'd have faced a defensive mother rather than one who was listening to what I had to say. At the same time, how could I allow a college-bound senior to have his papers partially written and almost entirely formulated by someone else? How would he learn independence of thought and skill?

> ### Voices from the Classroom
>
> I learned the definition of plagiarism in fifth grade. The piece I produced was six pages long; it was a work I now shudder to read, but it was a creation of my own imagination. Several days after turning my story in, I was called out of science class by my English teacher. She held the pages of my story in one hand and a pen in the other. She selected a circled word from one of the sheets; "Josephine, what does *cerulean* mean?" Flustered and confused, I blanked on the denotation but eventually muttered that cerulean is a shade of blue. The teacher laid my story on the desk, looked me right in the eye, and asked me with every nuance of accusation, "Josephine, do you know what plagiarism is? It's when you use work that is not your own and claim it for yourself. Now, tell me the truth—is this story your own creation?"
>
> "Yes," I replied, appalled by the question I had just been asked. Unsatisfied, my teacher wrote a lengthy letter on the last page of my story, "reminding" me of the definition and severity of committing plagiarism.
>
> *—Josephine, age sixteen*
>
> Josephine says that she "learned the definition of plagiarism" from the experience she describes. Besides the definition of the term one might find in a dictionary, what else do you think Josephine learned about plagiarism from this experience? What do you think Josephine's teacher was trying to accomplish in their meeting? Was she successful or unsuccessful?

Consider, for instance, an article from *The Boston Globe* on parent involvement in composing college essays:

> With the scramble to get into elite colleges at a fever pitch and with a rising number of educational consultants and college essay specialists ready to give students a competitive edge, admissions officers are keeping a sharp lookout for essays that might have had an undue adult influence. In some admissions offices, such submissions receive the dubious distinction DDI, short for "Daddy Did It." . . . The concern over heavy-handed adult involvement is mounting as the admissions essay has become a pivotal part of the application, a key way for students to stand out from the throngs of applicants with top grades and SAT scores. (Schworm 2008)

■ WRITE TO THE POINT

How often do you think parents of students at your school overinvolve themselves with assignments and student projects? Does that sort of over-involvement bother you, or is it irrelevant to you? Explain your answer.

_____

_____

_____

_____

_____

_____

Every English or social studies teacher I know has run across the paper that just sounds too good not because it was downloaded from the Internet but because a parent offered excessive help. And it's not just parents; your tutor, your grandmother, an older sibling, or, in some cases, even a former teacher may offer you too much help with the best of intentions.

So: how much help is too much?

Obviously, not only is getting your college-age cousin to write an essay for you by offering to do her laundry and then turning that paper in as your own wrong, but it's a bad idea; there's no guarantee that your cousin knows what your teacher wants or that she understands the material better than you do. On the other hand, getting *some* help isn't wrong at all. The book you're holding was edited and proofread by at least four or five other people. Editing isn't plagiarism.

I suggest that, when you share your written work with a parent or other adult, *you* dictate the terms of response. Here are some possibilities:

- Ask your reader simply to circle any problematic words, phrases, or sentences. Then see if you can figure out for yourself what issues that reader saw and work to correct them.

- Instead of having the reader make written notes, talk to him or her about the paper and make the notes yourself as you go.

- Provide the reader with the response checklist in Figure 3.3. The checklist is meant to encourage editing and help without allowing your reader to rewrite the paper for you. You could, of course, make a similar checklist of your own that focuses on other specific information that might be helpful for your writing process or for individual assignments.

> **Voices from the Classroom**
>
> I think the pressure to do well on what we are assigned leads to plagiarism. Pressure from parents, teachers, administration, colleges, and even pressure from our peers. People think I'm smart and I feel that I have to live up to that at times. I don't plagiarize unless there is no other way to get it done on my own, and if I do, it's really, really, really, really minor, like a sentence that I just change around.
>
> —Michael, age fourteen
>
> Take a look at Michael's last sentence. What do you make of his use of the word *really* four times in a row? Do you agree that changing a sentence around is minor? Why or why not?

Reasons? I'd Call Them Excuses

Near the beginning of this chapter is a top ten list. It includes reasons students commonly offer after they plagiarize; they're also ways in which students rationalize plagiarism to themselves. Go back and read that list. Is there really any good reason on it?

Even if you do your best to avoid plagiarism while you're writing, you may still find yourself caught in tricky situations. That's because some choices that lead to plagiarism occur long before you ever start to write or put together a final product. The next chapter deals with the early stages of approaching school assignments—research, notetaking, and your own ownership of the assignments you're given. It, too, gets at the heart of how you approach your own learning, so that, hopefully, you can move away from excuses and rationalizations and toward self-sufficiency as a student and a scholar.

Reader Response Checklist			
Writer's name:			
Reader's name:			
Assignment description:			
Date:			
How's my organization?	**Great job in this area!**	**Your work is fine in this area.**	**You might wish to work on this.**
Is my thesis clear and coherent?			
Is my introduction interesting?			
Does my conclusion sum up my ideas well?			
Have I organized my ideas in an appropriate order?			
Have I included all of the elements required by the assignment?			
How are my grammar and mechanics?			
Have I followed the rules for grammar?			
If not, where am I having trouble?			
Trouble spot 1:			
Trouble spot 2:			
Is my spelling correct?			
How's my writing style?			
Are my sentences varied and interesting?			
Do I choose my words well?			
How's the content of my piece?			
Is my paper interesting, creative, and original?			
Do I use ample evidence and examples to support my point?			

Figure 3.3

■ CASE STUDY: SUMMARY JUDGMENT

Andrew, a seventeen-year-old student, told me the following story:

> In eighth grade, I was an A student, but I hated my English teacher; the homework seemed dull and pointless. The assignment was to write summaries of each chapter—no analysis, just summary for the sole, express point of making sure we read the book. I decided I could out-smart the system. I went to a lesser-known website and turned in the chapter summaries completely plagiarized. About halfway through *To Kill a Mockingbird,* the teacher caught me and another student who had decided to cheat in the same way.
>
> I was totally embarrassed and still deeply regret my decision to pla-giarize. However, I view that day as a turning point in my academic career; I started to work harder and have never *really* plagiarized again (apart from minor offenses from copying textbook material). I feel my decision to cheat was not because I lacked moral judgment or because I was not aware of what I was doing. I viewed the assignment as busy-work and above all else, the teacher failed to reward individual students who put effort into the assignment, which eliminated the incentive to work harder to get a better grade. . . . I think that if the school had decided to punish me more, the real reason not to cheat would have been lost to me. It would turn an offense that is illegal because it is steal-ing into an offense that is wrong only if you are caught by your school.

Talking Points

1. Why do you think Andrew felt compelled to tell me that he "hated" his English teacher and that the homework in the class was "dull and pointless"?

2. What would you have done in Andrew's place? Can you think of ways to approach Andrew's problem without resorting to plagiarism?

3. Read the last two lines of the story again. Why is Andrew glad that he wasn't punished *more*? What lesson do you think Andrew learned from his experience? Are there any lessons he might have learned but didn't?

4 *Copy That!*

Strategies for Avoiding Plagiarism

Many books about avoiding plagiarism are really books about how to write research papers. In the first few pages, they tell you why plagiarism is wrong—because, well, *it's wrong*—and then the rest of the book is taken up with basic rules about how to take notes, how to cite, and how to make a bibliography.

I hope this book is different. OK, sure, this chapter covers notetaking, citation, and bibliographies. But if that's all you're looking for, you'd be better off picking up *The Elements of Style*, by Strunk and White, and settling in for a tough but very useful read. What I want to impress on you is that avoiding plagiarism is a matter of making numerous small decisions. You make some of those decisions when you're actually doing the research and some when you're making your bibliography. Others are made when you choose a topic or when you decide you'd rather spend your spare afternoon visiting the library than munching on snickerdoodles and surfing YouTube.

As I've said before, avoiding plagiarism is as much a matter of deciding how you want to learn as it is a question of right and wrong. Take, for instance, the standard research project. If you went hunting for scary two-word phrases in schools, the clear winner for terror-inducing, knee-knocking, hand-wringing combination would be *research paper*. Students, teachers, and pretty much anyone who's ever gone to school will start to mew like a wounded cat when you bring the subject up. I've even met professional researchers who shudder at the memory of the research papers they had to write in high school; one can well imagine Archimedes giving up any thoughts about buoyancy or water displacement and just staying in the bathtub all day if he'd thought his experiments would have had to be accompanied by 150 perfectly filled out note cards, a formal outline, and an annotated bibliography.

Some students and teachers do love the research paper, of course; the structure and order appeals to them, perhaps. But far more dread it (yes,

YOU NEED TO KNOW: My Survey of Tennessee Students

In the summer of 2007 I surveyed a group of eighty high school sophomores and juniors from around seventy different Tennessee high schools. The survey produced some interesting information about student expectations and perceptions. Here are some of the results:

1. When I asked students what kinds of sources they were allowed to use on research papers:

   - 17 percent of students said they used online sources only (including print sources accessed online);

   - 25 percent of students said they used print sources only; and

   - 58 percent of students said they used a mix of print and online sources.

2. The student responses also yielded these statistics about research papers in their schools:

   - Sixty-five percent of the students had completed a research paper or project in their English classes during the previous year, while only 38 percent had written a research paper for a social studies class.

   - Of those who wrote a research paper for an English class, 67 percent focused on a historical event or current events issue, not on a particular text or group of texts (I include in this grouping papers on the life of an author without an analysis of that author's writing).

   - The average number of pages for research papers in English was 8.5, for social studies, 3.5.

3. In order, students listed as the most effective ways of learning about specific topics discussion, lectures (but only by dynamic and interesting teachers), narratives and fiction, primary documents, readings from textbooks, and research projects involving writing. That list suggests volumes to me about the antipathy students feel toward the traditional research project but doesn't dissuade me from feeling that research is a necessary skill for students to possess.

4. When asked how often their teachers actively discussed the differences in expectations for research papers by discipline (i.e., the difference between what an English teacher might expect from such a paper and what a science teacher might expect), 25 percent of students responded that teachers held such discussions often, 40 percent sometimes, and 35 percent rarely or never. In follow-up discussions, it became clear to me that such differences in expectations were a major source of frustration to many students.

How closely do the results from my survey mirror those you'd expect to find in your own school? In what ways do the results make you rethink the nature of research projects and your approach to them? What might you say to the teachers of these students if you were given the chance?

your teachers may dread the assignments they make and make them anyway). For students, the dread comes from the tedium involved with most research assignments. For teachers, the dread comes from the fact that students who view the assignment as a tedious chore will probably write some terrible papers. And those teachers know that *some* of their students are likely, under such circumstances, to resort to plagiarism.

But research skills are valuable to students and professionals in all sorts of fields, so teachers keep plugging away. This is where you come in. Let's assume that, by now, you're the sort of student who doesn't *want* to plagiarize, who might every so often fall behind or come under tremendous time pressures but who would really rather not cheat because you know, after all, that it is wrong, and not just because some author told you so. Let's even assume that you understand the many benefits of writing an original research paper, benefits such as learning

- knowledge about a particular subject or academic area
- information-retrieval skills
- the conventions and format of research-based writing
- what professional models of research and source analysis entail
- the challenges and benefits of structuring and writing an extensive composition
- how to integrate the ideas of others and your own ideas into a coherent, sustained argument

Yet with all of this knowledge and insight and with the best of intentions, you still just don't want to write the darn ten-page paper your history teacher assigned. So you find yourself awake at eleven o'clock the night before the thing is due scrambling to put together something, anything, that might get you a decent grade.

Blame your teacher if you want—the assignment is lousy, the steps should have been clearer, whatever—but it won't get you anywhere. What will get you somewhere is thinking more carefully about the process the next time around. What will get you on track the next time around is knowing how and when to cite information, how to take good notes that prepare you for citation, how to find information online more easily, and, perhaps most importantly, how to take ownership of assignments so that you no longer hate them.

This chapter's not only about research papers; much of what you'll read here applies to essays, projects, and assignments of all sorts. But much of it also covers assignments that involve some level of research, because they constitute the biggest minefield for students wishing to avoid plagiarism.

■ TALKING POINT

Describe the last research paper or project you had to complete. What about it seemed like the biggest obstacle to you before you started? How did you handle—or fail to handle—that obstacle? What can you learn from that experience that might help you the next time you face a similar task?

Out of Cite: The Skill of Attributing Information

Turabian. MLA. Chicago. APA. Harvard. You're probably familiar with at least one of these terms (they're all formats for citing research material), but just hearing the word may also make your knees start to shake. It's a list that often leaves a student looking like a cartoon character who just got an anvil dropped on his head, little stars or birds circling happily while he stares, dazed, into space.

No matter which citation method your school uses (mine, for instance, uses both MLA and Turabian), there are three questions you might ask about citing sources within a paper: How? When? And, of course, why?

I've noticed that research assignments tend to focus on the first of these questions far more than on the last, yet the first is probably the easiest to

TOP TEN: Ways to Encourage Your Own Originality During the Writing Process

1. *Ask your teacher about your sources.* Your teacher may have used the same assignment in previous years or may just know more about the source material than you do. If you're having trouble finding sources, ask for help.

2. *Double-check your sources.* Don't rely on your memory for quotations, citations, or other source information. Go back and double-check your paper carefully to make sure that your citations line up with your bibliography and that your bibliography lines up with actual sources.

3. *Collaborate wisely.* When you are allowed to collaborate, do so. Be careful about collaboration that's not within the rules created by the teacher, and ask what those rules are if you aren't certain.

4. *Color-code as you type.* As you type your paper, highlight sentences in various colors: one for lines that include a quotation, one for summary and paraphrase, and so on. Besides helping you go back and check your attribution, this will give you a clear idea of how often you use your sources and how many of your own ideas are included in the paper.

5. *Consider your audience.* Keep in mind that a critical review, a journal article, a research proposal, a website, and a newspaper feature all have slightly different audiences; discussing with your teacher how to write for such audiences not only helps you tweak papers in a way that may discourage you from copying but is also good preparation for a variety of future writing assignments.

6. *Minimize the stakes.* You can't always control how much of your grade is determined by one paper or assignment. You can, however, try to avoid situations in which your entire grade or some external award is determined by one huge assignment by doing well in other parts of a course, talking to teachers or parents about your expectations, and keeping yourself focused on the goal of learning as well as the goal of achieving high marks.

7. *Check the rubric carefully.* Make sure you understand how you'll be graded and what your teacher wants to see. This may alleviate some pressure and will give you a better chance of completing your work strategically.

8. *Get help for revision, but not too much.* Work with your parents, friends, or teachers on your revision, but be careful that you're still writing your own words and ideas.

9. *Break the process into pieces.* Keep your progress under control and don't fall behind. Make a schedule, list, or plan to help you stay on track.

10. *Use current sources.* The newer the sources, the less likely they are to show up in prefabricated essays. Avoid falling back on the most obvious sources, as well (Wikipedia probably doesn't belong in your term paper) and look for solid, scholarly articles that will give you good ideas and help you avoid even the facade of plagiarism.

answer. MLA, for instance, provides specific instructions for citing just about every type of source, all of which are based on the simple premise that in-text citations need to point clearly to bibliographical entries (which in turn point clearly to the original sources). If, for instance, I note that the author of *Writing Research Papers: A Complete Guide* advises students to avoid plagiarism by developing "personal notes full of [their] own ideas on a topic" that "synthesize the ideas of the authorities" (Lester 118), then it's fairly simple to figure out from information in the same source that I *must* include the name of the author and the page number on which the information can be found in my parenthetical note (as I've done) and that the parentheses should immediately follow the quotation (which they do). If I'm unsure about the format of the parenthetical citation or the bibliography entry that must accompany my quotation, I can find a model quickly and with little fuss at numerous online sites such as Easybib.com and Citationmachine.net.

In other words: the *how* is the easiest part of the equation. Sure, there are occasional sources that throw students (and me) for a loop— how to cite a text by one author that is quoted in an appendix by another that is included in an online version of an anthology, for instance. *That* formatting rule I'd have to look up carefully. But in general, citation and bibliography formatting is the easy part. So why are students reluctant to do it? Some possible answers:

- When you're asked to cite, you must interrupt what is fundamentally a creative process of composition with a menial and noncreative task.

- If you perceive that citation is difficult (or if you don't have any knowledge of appropriate citation procedure), you're more likely to avoid the exercise altogether.

- If citation seems to have no importance other than as a part of an eventual grade, your motivation for citing correctly will naturally be low.

- You may fear that citing sources will make your work seem less original.

Many teachers address citation issues mainly by distributing to students examples (or directing them to an online site that shows examples) of proper citation for the style used in the course. That's not bad practice—you need a clear guide, and many easily understandable guides of this sort exist. But a handout is not sufficient here; it doesn't clearly answer the when? or why? questions that the reasons for avoiding plagiarism I mentioned previously embody. I can play a simple scale on the piano all day long, but unless someone tells me why that exercise is valuable and when I might use the skill, I'll go watch *American Idol* instead.

By all means, go get a list of citation rules and follow it, but you also need to buy into citation if you're really going to learn to navigate those rules.

■ WRITE TO THE POINT

In the space below, list the citation rules you're most commonly expected to know for papers you write.

_____

_____

_____

_____

_____

_____

Now ask yourself: How certain are you of these rules? What areas of citation confuse you? How could you clear up any confusion you have about these rules, and are you likely to do so when necessary? If not, why not?

_____

_____

_____

_____

_____

_____

Timing Is Everything: When and How to Cite

Let's face it; if you're going to write a book about plagiarism and originality, you've got to be pretty darn careful to get your source material correct. I've tried hard to do that in this book, but it's no small challenge. When I write, sometimes I work on a computer at school, sometimes at home, and most often at the local coffee shop (people ask me how in the world I can work in public like that, but compared with the environment created by the two kids I have at home or the one created by the two hundred at school, a coffee shop is a blissful oasis). I don't use note cards; I keep track of URLs, titles, and authors in a spreadsheet file. My school librarian helps me obtain books, but I do use a lot of Internet sources. While writing this book, I often worked on multiple chapters at once— *and* this wasn't the only piece I was writing at the time.

No, I'm not trying to elicit tears on my behalf; I'm just making the point that if I've worked harder than ever to be sure my source material is correct and still struggled with the simple *logistics* of it all, I can imagine the feelings you have when compiling a major research paper, with sources you've grabbed from three different libraries and six different computers. How do you keep track?

> **Voices from the Classroom**
>
> I cannot say how many people have explained to me what plagiarism is and what it is not, or how many different versions I've heard. They all say plagiarism is using someone's ideas without giving them credit. Then why have teachers said if you list a source in the bibliography and don't cite it internally that you are plagiarizing? The source is in the works cited; you've given it credit. . . . The problem lies in the fact that everyone has a different set of rules for plagiarism. This is frustrating, confusing, and leads to accidental plagiarism.
>
> —*Allison, age sixteen*
>
> Do you ever feel the same frustration as Allison about expectations involving plagiarism? What experiences have you had that created similar confusion?

In the simplest terms, I want you to construct the following for yourself, as I have:

1. a system and routine for keeping track of source material;

2. an internal sense of when to cite (based on the rules of the appropriate citation format);

3. a knowledge of basic citation rules, with the ability to unearth the complicated ones as necessary; and

4. an understanding of the ethics of attribution.

The three following sections cover note taking (system), decisions about when and how to cite (the internal sense), and citation format (rules). As you read them, consider the process you use for researching papers and projects.

Take Note: Preparing the Way for Citation

The simple fact of the matter is that most teachers instruct students to take research notes as they themselves were taught to take research notes. For most teachers, that amounts to a simple formula: note cards.

There's a good reason for this, too: note cards worked for many generations of students and teachers. Those teachers who continue to use them mean to offer their students a system for capturing vital information about a source. Consider the two examples of the traditional note card from a real tenth grader's research paper on the poet Elizabeth Bishop in Figure 4.1.

Though particulars vary, the form of these note cards, dictated by the student's teacher, more or less reflects the traditional manner of taking notes: one card contains a single piece of information with a link to the source card; the second contains the necessary information to format a bibliographical entry for the source. Most teachers who require note cards have students collect their notes on multiple cards, then arrange them according to an outline and use them to compose the final paper.

I'm not out to bash teachers who still require note cards, and I've heard some reasonable defenses of the practice (first and foremost, note cards pretty clearly demonstrate to you exactly what information is required to cite properly). At the same time, I recall my own friend in

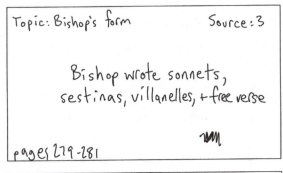

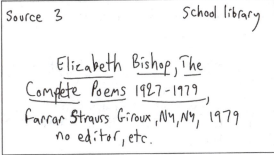

Figure 4.1

ninth grade, who fabricated *every* note card for a paper that required us to compile more than one hundred of them. I'll bet that you have similar stories. There was little chance, back then, that the teacher would catch him—the Internet didn't exist and we were allowed to visit the public library to collect sources, so tracking down the sources themselves would have required considerable effort.

To an Internet age student like you, note cards may seem as quaint as vinyl records or those early cell phones that were about the size of a loaf of bread. I showed the note cards from Figure 4.1 to a class of high school seniors who were currently working on thirty-page literary analysis papers. All twenty students had completed significant research for their paper without any particular guidance from their teacher as to the form their notes must take; of the twenty, none had used note cards like those I showed them, at least not since middle school. So how did they take notes? By

- bookmarking websites in their Internet browsers
- printing or photocopying source material
- keeping a list of URLs in Word or Excel, with annotations

- making notes on electronic sticky notes (notes that appeared on their computer's desktop) using a free program

- remembering and making note of the keywords they used to search for material online

- returning to the online catalog of libraries, from which they could access all information about their sources

- saving files from electronic journal collections such as JSTOR or Questia.com

- simply inserting quotations as they wrote the paper using a cut-and-paste method and immediately entering bibliographic material into a saved file on a site such as Easybib.com

■ WRITE TO THE POINT

In the space below, describe the system you typically use when you complete research for a paper or project. How do you keep track of sources? Are you satisfied with this system? Why or why not?

_____

_____

_____

_____

_____

One girl I spoke to just laughed when I asked her whether note cards wouldn't be a more certain system. "Do I look like I *want* to waste my time handwriting all that information and then retyping it when I can do it with about two clicks?" she asked. But what about the possibilities for shuffling and reorganizing notes? She shrugged. "What do you think a mouse is for?"

Whole books could be written about note taking, but for our purposes, let's refocus on a single objective: you need to take good notes while researching so that you won't plagiarize. I'll agree that note cards are probably a pain you'd rather avoid if you'll agree that you still need a system for taking notes. Here, then, are two mnemonics I recommend as alternative methods to help make notes more effective and to deter plagiarism:

CAPITAL IDEA

The unfortunate part of this acronym is that the letters don't fall absolutely in order of importance, but they are all intended to remind students of important pieces of information—the pieces they'll likely need before using the source in a paper. The full version:

City—the city where the work was published (if a print source)

Author of the work

Page—page number or specific part of a site where the information can be found

Information—the salient quotation, fact, or idea that will be used by the student

Title—again, of a print source or web page (for magazines and journals, this includes volume and edition number)

Annotation—personal notes about the source, its usefulness, and how it might help the student

Location—where was the source found? In a library, at a URL?

Internet host—or publisher of a print source

Date—when was the source published or last updated?

Edition—or volume number of a journal or magazine

Access—the date on which a website was accessed

Some sources, of course, require a slightly different approach (a speech or interview, for instance). Some might not require all of this information. Note, too, that this mnemonic leans toward Internet usage, but it includes the information most often needed to cite print sources, as well.

■ TALKING POINT

Look at the CAPITAL IDEA list of information again. Why do you think this particular information is important to those who read your work? Is there any information on the list that seems unimportant to you, or are there items that seem important that you think are missing from the list? What judgments about a source—especially an online source—could you make or not make based on this information alone?

Now, here's the second mnemonic:

CHoMP

The CHoMP note-taking strategy was published in the *English Journal* by Kathleen Guinee and Maya B. Eagleton, who described it as "one solution for teaching students to transform information into knowledge" and as a response to "an alarming number of students" who "unwittingly plagiarize large portions of their final research products" (2006, 46). The simple version:

Cross out small words, such as prepositions and conjunctions.

Highlight important information in the remaining text.

Make notes based on the highlighted information by abbreviating, truncating, making lists, using symbols, and drawing instead of writing full sentences.

Put the notes into your own words.

As a sample, Figure 4.2 contains a passage from Guinee and Eagleton's original article with steps 1 and 2, crossing out and highlighting, completed.

Step 3, note making, might look like Figure 4.3.

And step 4, rewriting, might look like Figure 4.4.

I find CHoMP quite helpful. Eventually, of course, the object should be to move past such step-by-step approaches, which slow down the

---

Based on our research experiences, we think the CHoMP strategy has promise for helping students to paraphrase source documents and avoid plagiarism in their research projects. However, students still need literacy foundations and additional strategies for producing high-quality research products. (51)

Figure 4.2

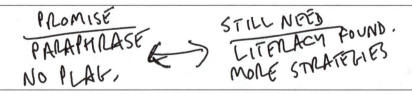

Figure 4.3

The CHoMP strategy, its authors assert, might help students paraphrase and keep from plagiarizing, but those same authors recognize the need for other approaches to research and writing for most students.

Figure 4.4

research process in the interest of careful attention to originality. In order to do that, you must internalize the note-taking process more and more; CHoMP is a good first step in that direction.

■ TALKING POINTS

1. How useful is the CHoMP system, in your opinion? Can you think of ways you accomplish the same goals and yet shorten the steps involved here? If so, how? Would you as be comfortable with those shortcuts as you would be using the CHoMP system?

2. Discuss exactly how *not* taking good notes could lead students to plagiarize. What challenges might students without good notes encounter during the writing process?

A Fine Balance: How Much, How Often, from How Many Sources?

There's no strict answer to how often you should quote or cite in a paper. The answer I'd *like* to give to the question, "How many sources should I use?" is, of course, "As many as you need" (substitute *pages* or *cups of coffee* or *camels* for the word *sources* and, depending on the task at hand, the answer is just as tempting). But for most students, that answer isn't very satisfying.

When students ask how many quotations or citations they should have, I start by describing a basic pyramid structure for papers (see Figure 4.5), in which every important point is supported by at least two sources or quotations; the structure works whether one is writing a two-page essay on *Julius Caesar* or a five-page research paper on Caesar's conquest of Gaul.

One can also imagine expanding this model indefinitely by adding more supporting ideas or dividing supporting ideas into even smaller units of support; one could also, for good measure, increase the number of sources or quotations necessary to support each point.

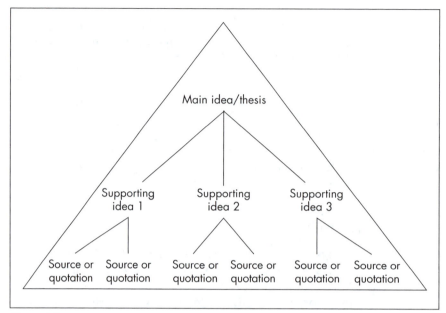

Figure 4.5

It's not an organic process of research, but it's a place to begin. Other general guidelines you might consider for the research papers you write:

- one source overall for each page of a research paper (e.g., a five-page paper requires at least five sources)
- at least two citations for each page of a research paper (e.g., a five-page paper requires at least ten citations)

Even better, though, is to ask yourself questions such as those that follow. The idea is to reflect critically on your own research to make sure you've done the best you can in addressing the topic you've been assigned.

- Have I included enough evidence to support my points?
- Have I cited all of the sources that deserve credit for the ideas I've presented?
- Are my sources varied, reputable, and balanced?
- Would a reader see a trend in my sources that might raise questions about my process?

- Are my sources evenly distributed throughout the section? If not, is there a valid reason why not?

- Have I clearly and sufficiently explained the quotations and sources I used, including establishing a context for each source's authenticity or relationship to the topic?

- Are there types of sources (or specific sources) that a reader would expect to see in my paper that aren't there?

A Method in the Madness: Learning Citation Formats

Let's say you want to quote this sentence in your research paper. What information would you include in your citation? It depends on the format (see Figure 4.6).

Figure 4.6 shows the simplest format: citing the source at the end of the sentence. But now imagine the variations on citing the sentence using MLA format alone:

- One writer asks us to imagine quoting "this sentence in your research paper" (Gilmore 61).

- Gilmore asks us to imagine quoting "this sentence in your research paper" (61).

> ### Voices from the Classroom
>
> My history teacher asks these questions, like, "How many people like cheese?" And the textbook says, "60 percent of people like cheese." How do you not plagiarize that? But then she gets mad if I copy from the book. And on her essays, it's not like you'd look it up on the Internet, but they're fact based. But then last year's history teacher allowed us to copy up to three words from the text, and my freshman teacher gave all opinion essays and diary entries that you couldn't plagiarize. It's all stuff I could copy if I want; I *try* to do it myself, but sometimes it's just impossible.
>
> —*Darlene, age sixteen*
>
> Have you ever been given an assignment you felt actually encouraged you to plagiarize? If so, how'd you deal with it? If you received such an assignment today, what options would you have that might increase your chances at avoiding plagiarism?

Format	In-Text Citation	Used Mainly By
MLA	(Gilmore 61)	English and languages
APA or Harvard	(Gilmore, 2008, 61)	social and physical sciences
Chicago or Turabian	footnotes or endnotes	history and related fields

Figure 4.6

- Gilmore refers to using his own sentence "in your research paper" (61) at the start of one section of his book.

- Educator Barry Gilmore poses this thought:

  Let's say you want to quote this sentence in your research paper. What information would you include in your citation? (61)

And we've not even discussed the difficulties of bibliographical formats yet. Asking you to juggle these rules in your head just for the sake of it is crazy. I recommend looking online for a very specific style sheet or online resource to use as reference while you format papers. There's also an appendix at the end of this book that includes basic citation rules for various formatting systems you might be asked to use.

■ WRITE TO THE POINT

In the space below, list any subjects in which you're expected to cite sources and the citation format you're expected to use for each. If you're not certain which formats your teachers wish you to use for certain subjects, indicate your uncertainty by writing "don't know."

_____

_____

_____

_____

_____

Now consider your list. How often might a student in your school be expected to switch between formats? What reasons might your teachers offer for requiring you to switch formats? If you can, discuss your answers with your teacher or classmates.

_____

_____

_____

_____

Start Your Engines: Searching for Information Online

When I typed the word *plagiarism* into Google, the first two sites the search engine returned were Plagiarism.org, a site maintained by the same company that owns Turnitin.com, and Wikipedia's entry on *plagiarism*. When I typed the word into Google Scholar, the first site returned was a chapter of an online book titled "Borrowing Others' Words: Text, Ownership, Memory, and Plagiarism," by Alastair Pennycook; at the time, you could read some, but not all, of the chapter in the online version.

If you know a few basic search rules and commands, you'll be able to navigate the sea of information online more readily. A few examples can be found in Figure 4.7 (which also, not surprisingly, led me to the discovery that very little has been posted online about the role of monkeys in cases of plagiarism).

You type this . . .	The search engine looks for sites that . . .
plagiarism monkeys	mention plagiarism and monkeys in any way
plagiarism and monkeys	contain information about *both* plagiarism and monkeys
plagiarism and not monkeys	contain information about plagiarism but not about monkeys
plagiarism or monkeys	contain information about either plagiarism or monkeys
"plagiarism and monkeys"	use the exact phrase "plagiarism and monkeys" at some point
+title "plagiarism" and monkeys	are titled "Plagiarism" and contain some mention of monkeys
domain:edu and plagiarism and monkeys	are hosted by a domain ending in .edu (or whatever domain you specify) and include information about plagiarism and monkeys

Figure 4.7

Narrowing the options of a search is a useful trick, but also remember the arbitrary nature of such engines. Pages are ranked by search engines in a variety of ways; the information for which you're searching doesn't always come up in the first ten hits out of six hundred thousand. Smart searching means trying a number of different phrasings, keywords, and search options; it also means taking the time to follow links and delve into web content in more than a cursory manner.

The following methods may help you remember some tricks for smarter searching.

SEARCH

I wouldn't want to attack the Internet armed with nothing but a vague topic such as "plagiarism" or "monkeys" any more than I'd want to send my six-year-old daughter into a candy store with a thousand dollars. The possible options for return information are staggering. But when you are likely to start a search and come across a large amount of material, one strategy I like uses the acronym SEARCH: search, examine, assemble, return, collect, harvest. Here are the steps:

Search for a topic using an advanced search engine (such as Google Scholar). You may like to start with a general search using a search engine or Wikipedia to familiarize yourself with a topic. That's fine, but when it's time to find usable source material, try beginning with a narrow search that will yield not just immediate information but bibliographic links and reputable sources right off the bat.

Examine reputable sources and follow links to major journal archives and other sources, for instance:

- JSTOR
- Questia
- eNotes
- Google Book Search
- Amazon book previews
- FindArticles.com

Many of the articles you find through this kind of advanced search are archived through online sites that require registration. However, you can often access a preview, abstract, or excerpt, and often enough the full text is available as well. Make a note of promising articles that are not easily accessible for later reference.

Assemble a source list from bibliographies, notes, and references. One of the most valuable lessons I learned as a student was how to follow the trail of a bibliography. Note the sources one writer uses, look those sources up, and then check the bibliography for other sources that might also be useful.

Return to a search engine to look for specific items. Having found a potentially useful title in a bibliography, it's often worthwhile simply to cut and paste that title into a search engine and run a broad search for an online text. Often, for instance, the author of an article will post a copy on a personal website.

Collect more search keywords (and more sources). The process can be repeated, but along the way you'll probably learn more ways to narrow the search. You might begin researching by typing the term *plagiarism* or *cheating* into the search engine, for instance, but as you investigate phrases like *academic dishonesty*, names like McCabe and Howard, and potential sources such as the *Chronicle of Higher Education* will come up again and again; noting these recurring terms, you can then refine your search accordingly.

Harvest an original bibliography of reputable sources (and go to the library!). If you go online or to a library armed with a list of titles, you're far ahead of the game; eventually, this process of checking and rechecking keywords and bibliographies and of using a variety of search options will result in a useful bibliography.

CARS

On his website, Virtualsalt.com, author Robert Harris (2007) offers this quick reference guide students might use to evaluate Internet resources. The acronym CARS makes it easy to remember.

Credibility—author's credentials, evidence of quality control. Indicators of lack of credibility: anonymous sites, lack of contradictory points of view, bad grammar.

Accuracy—timeliness, comprehensiveness, audience awareness. Indicators of lack of accuracy: out-of-date, incomplete, or overly general information, information that can't be corroborated from other sources.

Reasonableness—fairness, objectivity. Indicators of lack of reasonableness: clear biases, slanted tone, conflicts of interest.

Support—documentation, external objectivity. Indicators of lack of support: no references to sources or other sites, no contact information or "about us" page, no citations.

I speak to students frequently about the need not just for useful sources but for reputable ones—Wikipedia, for instance, useful as it is, contains plenty of misinformation, since it is composed entirely of material submitted by users around the world regardless of their credentials, background, or expertise. (I recently noticed that the article on my own school listed President George W. Bush and Michael Jackson as alumni; neither is true.) Though I won't tell you never to visit Wikipedia, I also encourage you not to rely on it as a source; it may guide your research but not act as research in its own right. Harris' mnemonic is a useful guide for determining which websites you should or shouldn't include in your own bibliographies.

The Attribution Solution: Considering *Why* to Cite

"Why does citation matter?"

The question hangs in the air of my Advanced Placement (AP) class for a few seconds before anyone ventures an answer.

Finally, Rafael raises his hand warily. "Because you'll fail us if we don't do it?"

"OK," I say. "What else?"

Another student, Janet, shrugs. "You've got to say where your sources come from."

"How come?" I ask.

"So someone else can find them, I guess. But I don't think that really matters much in *my* papers. It's just, like, practice."

Janet's got a point, and I don't have a great response handy, because with the particular paper we're discussing, it's not likely anyone else will try to find her sources. But this is a sort of practice, practice for later assignments that will matter a lot in Janet's professional or academic life, and I want her to understand that it's about other people finding the information and more.

Look: We've talked about why you shouldn't plagiarize or cheat. But why *should* you attribute the information you find? Here are a few reasons I offered Janet's class:

- Plagiarism defeats the main point of writing assignments: learning to think critically and analyze.

- When a student fails to cite, it destroys trust in the academic setting. It's a lot harder to regain trust than it is to lose it.

- Plagiarism and the failure to attribute material cheat the reader; they make it impossible to follow a trail of sources and to track down ideas.

- A plagiarized source is often impossible to track down again when the author wants to find more information.

■ TALKING POINT

How closely do you agree—or to what extent do you disagree—with the four reasons for avoiding plagiarism listed here? Can you think of any other reasons not to plagiarize that your class might add to this list? In your opinion, which of the reasons above is the best reason not to plagiarize and why?

Note that I didn't include consequences or punishments as part of this list; we've covered that already. Citation goes beyond the ethics of stealing and the rules of your school. When you cite, you become part of a discussion with readers—teachers, other students, scholars. Cheapen that discussion, and you cheapen your own ability to learn.

Which leads us to the first step of avoiding plagiarism. It happens before you ever start to write, before you take notes, and even before you search for sources. It happens when you first hear about an assignment, when you decide how to approach that assignment, and when you either take ownership of it or let it own you.

Taking It Back: Owning the Assignments You're Given

It would be wonderful if teachers let you choose the books you'd read, the type of papers you'd write, the projects you'd complete, or even the topics you'd address in homework and other assignments. It doesn't work that way often enough, I think, and it makes it tough for you to learn at your own rate and in the ways that work for you best. Sometimes, of course, your teachers know what you need to learn and how you can get there, sometimes it's just easier for them to make the assignments they've always made, and sometimes they make assignments because they're worried that students who aren't given specific guidelines are more likely to cheat.

There are other times when you do get a choice. School science fairs often work this way. Sometimes teachers allow students to choose topics for research papers. Personal essays and creative writing assignments open up doors for your own originality. I hope you seize these opportunities when you're given the chance. Choice is a great way to increase your desire to complete a project, but only if you take advantage of the times you're offered a choice. If you fall back on a science fair topic because it's all you can think of at the last minute, you're dooming yourself to boredom—and inching yourself that much closer toward the kinds of bad choices that lead some students to copy their work.

■ WRITE TO THE POINT

In the space below, describe any assignments given in your classes in which you have a choice in how you complete your work. Then write a sentence or two describing your attitude toward those assignments compared with others you're given. Are you more engaged when you complete those assignments, less engaged, or engaged about as much either way? Do you tend to perform better, worse, or about the same when you have a choice? Explain your answers.

_____

_____

_____

_____

_____

_____

_____

So how do you take ownership? Here are some suggestions you might consider:

- *Make assignments personally relevant when you can*. If your grandparents immigrated from Australia, why not write that social studies report about Aborigines or kangaroos? Who knows? You might learn something interesting and increase your chances of caring about the paper at the same time.

- *Research your choices.* I well remember getting stuck with a research paper topic in tenth-grade history that I couldn't have cared less about—something to do with price inflation during the Great Depression—simply because I couldn't be bothered to look up some of the topics I didn't really know much about. In retrospect, I might not have bombed that assignment if I'd known how interesting I'd find a topic such as the Bay of Pigs (in my tenth-grade ignorance, I envisioned *that* paper as being all about farm animals). A little research before choosing a topic would have gone a long way.

- *Expand topics and look for alternate ways to answer questions and prompts.* Can you write your chemistry report on the periodic table in first person instead of third? Can you format your report on ancient Roman sacrifices like a newspaper article? Are you allowed to argue that Ma is the true hero of *Grapes of Wrath*? Until you talk to your teacher, you'll never know—and the answer just might encourage you to dive into the assignment with new enthusiasm.

- *Allow yourself to become interested in something new.* This sounds silly at first, but you'd be surprised how many students (and adults) think they know what they are and aren't interested in before they actually know anything about the topic. Back in tenth grade, if I'd allowed myself, I might have discovered some really interesting things about the economy during the Great Depression, but I was so dead set on hating the paper that I never even gave it a chance.

- *Break a process into pieces (and choose which parts you tackle first).* Large projects are overwhelming. Heck, sometimes writing a few sentences is overwhelming. But if you break the assignment down and start it with your original thoughts and style, you're far more likely to complete it on your own, as well. Start with the part of the process you like most—or with the part you really hate. Either way, once you've begun, you're that much more likely to keep going without falling back on shortcuts.

What I said at the start of this book is still true: plagiarism is easy. If avoiding plagiarism were just a matter of knowing the right rules, it would be easy, too. Avoiding plagiarism, though, is a matter of knowing the right rules *and* organizing yourself to use that knowledge. It's a matter of recognizing the value of learning, the value of the rules, and the pressures the system will put on you as you work.

■ CASE STUDY: TWO OF A KIND

A colleague of mine—a college professor—shared this story with me:

My last experience with plagiarism was complex. Two students turned in papers that shared about 40 percent of the same material. The phrasings were identical, but their placement in the paper differed. They also included the same irrelevant material that didn't really have anything to do with the topic. One of the papers was pretty good, otherwise. The other was pretty lousy. Finally, there were a few sentences lifted word for word from the textbook, but just two or so.

I did a Web search or five. I typed the repeating paragraphs into Turnitin.com. I couldn't find any external source.

So, I called each student in and spoke to them independently. The first claimed that they studied together and put together notes, and then he wrote his paper from notes which must have been the same as his peer's notes. He couldn't produce said notes.

The second said much the same thing, but also said that he wrote his paper first and let his friend look at it. When confronted, the first said he had never seen his friend's paper. Later, he came back and said that he had written his paper first and then had gone to bed at about 4 A.M. with his friend still not having written.

Talking Points

1. If you found yourself in this teacher's position, what would you do? Fail both students? Fail one student but not the other? Require both to rewrite the assignment? Ignore the problem altogether? What possible drawbacks and benefits might each reaction have for these students and for others in the course?

2. The professor points out that one or two sentences in each paper were taken directly from the textbook for the class. In your mind, is this plagiarism a greater or lesser offense than copying the majority of the paper from a peer? Explain your answer.

3. Besides the possible decision to plagiarize, what other poor decisions were made by the students in the story? How do you feel these decisions contributed to their ultimate confrontations with the professor?

4. Besides failing, what possible consequences might these students face in the course, in other courses, or in their relationships because of the decisions they made regarding this assignment?

5 *Making It Personal*

Plagiarism and the Culture of Your School

Think for a moment about this information, which comes from a study summarized in an article titled "Students Plagiarize Less than Many Think, a New Study Finds":

> 24.5 percent of students reported "often," "very frequently," or "sometimes" having cut and pasted text from the Internet without proper citation. . . . Meanwhile, more than 90 percent of students reported that their peers "often," "very frequently," or "sometimes" copied text without citation from conventional sources. (Kellogg 2002)

Did you notice that second sentence? Far more students *think* that plagiarism happens all the time than actually *admit* to plagiarizing. And sure, a few probably just aren't willing to admit it. But what if a survey revealed that one-quarter of students claim to drink coffee each day, while 90 percent of students believe that all of their friends drink coffee? Which number would you believe?

■ TALKING POINT

How would you describe the frequency of plagiarism at your school? How do most students and teachers perceive the problem? How might a gap between the actual frequency of plagiarized papers and the perceived frequency affect decisions by individual students or teachers?

Culture makes a difference in the decisions we make. If it's cool to claim you pulled an all-nighter at your school, aren't some people more likely to get tired at midnight but keep studying anyway? Haven't you heard the "everyone does it" excuse from students who break rules in other areas of school? Similarly, if the students in a school think that everyone else is getting ahead by plagiarizing, won't it be easier to rationalize dishonesty?

I'm not saying that peer pressure is impossible to resist. But plagiarism keeps happening—both in schools and in professional areas such as politics, academic writing, and show business—even though most people consider it to be wrong.

This chapter contains information drawn from studies of several aspects of school life. The goal is not to blame your school for plagiarism, but to help you think about how you navigate the daily expectations school places on you—and to help you prepare to meet those expectations. There are no easy answer to dealing with the challenges of grades, reward systems, honor codes, sports, gender, collaborative assignments, or other facets of schooling, but perhaps the information that follows can offer some first steps in that direction.

Making the Grade: Rankings and Grades in Middle and High School

"Tell me why you got an A on that writing assignment," I say to one of my better students; call her Melanie.

"I did everything the teacher asked," Melanie answers. "I used the right number of sources, I wrote it long enough, and I didn't make any mistakes."

"That's *how*," I say. "Does that answer *why*?"

Melanie considers this for a moment. "Well, it tells me why the teacher gave me an A, I guess. She wanted me to learn to do it right."

"What about content? Did she grade you on the quality of your ideas?"

"Yeah, I think so," she says.

"How do you know?"

Melanie shows me the essay. "She wrote, 'good thinking and originality,' at the top. Then she just marked the rubric that says I did everything right."

"OK, so why did you do everything right?"

"To get an A."

"What about good thinking and originality?" I ask.

> ### Voices from the Classroom
>
> Long ago, I realized that I care more about receiving good grades than actually learning. Even though I realize this is wrong, that knowledge should be more important than report cards, I cannot seem to change my attitude. As a straight A student who aims one day to be valedictorian, I want good grades whether I deserve them or not.
>
> Quite frankly, I do blame the system. The competitiveness, the honoring of principal's list students, the prestige—it all just encourages students to get good grades by any means necessary. Everything is a grade, and grades are all people see.
>
> —*Ainsley, age sixteen*
>
> How closely do you agree with Ainsley's attitude? What role do you think "the system" plays in pressuring students to make higher grades?

Melanie frowns. "Well, I think I did OK, but really I just answered the question. I know what's on the rubric, though, and I know that I have to do the sources and all that to get a top grade. That's what I care about most."

"How come?" I ask.

"College. And my parents. And I just feel good when I get an A."

"Would you ever cheat to get an A?"

"No," Melanie answers. "But I know a whole lot of people who would."

■ WRITE TO THE POINT

Do you tend to get more feedback from your teachers when you make an A or when you make a lower grade? Does the length of teacher response change the way you react to your grades? When you make a higher grade, do you always feel that it means you've learned more? Write your answers to any or all of these questions, with explanations, in the space below.

_____

_____

_____

_____

_____

What strikes me about the conversation with Melanie is the fact that she's not fully convinced about her own learning. Grades are important to her and learning is a desirable but casual by-product of achieving those grades. She's comfortable operating in a system that is built to allow her to achieve those grades with hard work. For Melanie and many other students, assuming you follow all of the rules of the assignment, the harder you work, the higher your grade should be.

As a teacher, I can pretty easily imagine some students resorting to cheating in a system like this. First of all, cheating bypasses all of that hard work. But even more to the point, there are probably a lot of students out there who work very hard and receive lower scores on assignments than students who don't have to try all that much, and that can be really frustrating.

Now consider another study, this one by psychologist Eric M. Anderman. He found that students who cheat tend to

- worry about school
- perceive their school as focused on grades and ability
- believe they can obtain some kind of reward for doing well in class
- attribute failure in school to outside circumstances
- avoid using deep-level cognitive process strategies, such as trying different ways to solve a problem (APA 1998)

The middle three findings in the list have to do, mostly, with attitude, and attitude can certainly affect the decisions you make. But the first and last have to do with your ability to learn. If you're spending your time worrying about school, you're not spending that time actually learning the material—you can get an A on a history assignment about Augustus Caesar without actually internalizing any lessons about leadership or military strategy, for instance.

The last point is the one that really bothers me, however. There's an important element of this point to note: the study doesn't tell us only that students who cheat don't learn from the particular assignment on which they cheat (no surprise there). The study tells us that students who cheat tend not to think as deeply *even when they're not cheating*. Such students simply don't get in the habit of learning strategically; they focus on how to get a grade, not on how to learn the material.

■ TALKING POINT

What rewards do students in your school receive for doing well? Do these rewards tend to reinforce learning or just making higher grades? Do you think some students would cheat in order to obtain these rewards? Explain your answers.

I accept that grades are an important part of your life as a student, and I won't try to tell you that they're not. I do, though, want you to keep them in perspective. Grades are *not* the same thing as learning. If, ultimately, learning is at all important to you, then avoiding plagiarism should be important, too.

Here are a few suggestions to keep your focus on learning without sacrificing your grades:

- *Take risks.* Imagine that your English teacher tells you to write an essay arguing that Hamlet is a tragic hero. You might believe that Hamlet isn't a tragic hero, and you could try arguing that. But you might stretch the point even further—you might argue that Ophelia, Hamlet's girlfriend, is the real tragic hero. You might argue that there's no tragic hero, or that Hamlet is actually the villain, or that Hamlet is the tragic hero in acts 1, 2, and 3 and that Laertes (Ophelia's brother) is the tragic hero in acts 4 and 5. The same approach holds true for proving a scientific hypothesis or solving a word problem in math: question the question itself, take risks in your answer, and you'll probably not only do a better job on the assignment (ideally, making a better grade and learning at the same time) but also actually enjoy working on it.

- *Talk to your teacher before starting an assignment.* This approach is partly a matter of self-defense; you don't want to fail an assignment for not following the rules. If you're going to argue that Romeo is evil, you might want to run the idea by your English teacher (who more than likely adores the guy) first. But there's more to it than that; your teacher can help you think about the assignment and its solutions differently, she can tell you what probably won't work, and she can explain the grading procedures she'll use more thoroughly so that you can learn and achieve at the same time.

- *Learn strategically.* To some extent, learning strategically has to do with not taking shortcuts; the quickest route to completing an assignment is not always the one that teaches you the most. But more than that, students who learn strategically tend to take control of their own learning, from the way they take notes to the topics they choose for essays and projects. Many students are encouraged to develop good study habits that involve *working* strategically; learning is a bit different.

- *Revise your work.* Often, more learning happens in revision than it does in the initial creation. Some teachers require revision, but even when they don't, setting aside enough time to complete a rough draft and a final draft—possibly with some appropriate input from others in between—is a good idea for any major assignment. Outlining your ideas on paper is another solid step toward original thinking. Such planning steps also help relieve the pressure that leads some students to plagiarize.

- *Ask your teachers about your writing and other work.* If you think about it, no one could comment on one hundred homework assignments and not get tired. You don't need to be a pest, but it's worthwhile to speak to your teachers—once in a while—to see what they have to say about your progress. In some cases, this will help you improve, but even if you make an A on six papers in a row, talking to the teacher may give you some ideas about how to improve your skills even if the changes don't affect your grades. It's a good idea, of course, to schedule such discussions in advance and not to expect life-changing responses from every meeting, but you might occasionally be surprised at what teachers have to say out loud that they didn't have the time or energy to write at the top of the page.

- *Don't worry about the honor roll.* Easier said than done? Sure. And it's nice to see your name on that list, or on any similar list that rewards achievements. But the honor roll should be symbolic of the amount you've learned; it shouldn't be the goal itself but the recognition that you've worked toward the real goal—learning.

- *Don't get caught up in extrinsic rewards.* I've heard of every kind of reward from pizza parties to cash for students who made high grades. Parents, teachers, and administrators sometimes offer such incentives with the best of intentions, and I don't begrudge you the items you can get for your achievement. As with grades and the honor roll, however, such rewards are not the most important result of hard work in school.

- *Don't use learning as an excuse.* None of the advice I offer here is meant to release you from your obligation to complete school assignments to the best of your ability; just because grades don't always reflect learning, don't allow yourself to make that into an excuse for not earning better grades. In the best of all possible worlds, you (along with your teachers, parents, or other interested adults) can combine learning and achievement without immense pressure.

Voices from the Classroom

Supposedly, high school is about learning. However, since no kid actually had the choice to go of his own free will, many do not feel that academic integrity matters. No college-bound student will deny, though, that grades matter a lot. The majority of the time kids work for the grade not the knowledge. How often does one hear, "Yes, I memorized the preamble to the Declaration!" rather than "Yes, I got an A!"

Personally, I care more about the grade than the knowledge. Much of the stuff I supposedly learn has little practical value, whereas grades are my future.

—*Ryan, age fifteen*

Ryan suggests that he learns little of "practical value" in high school courses. Do you feel the same way? What response might one of Ryan's teachers make to his comments, and how closely would you agree with that teacher?

May I Have the Honor? Thinking About Honor Codes

Your school may or may not have an honor code. Most of them work like this: The school tells you to write a pledge on your papers (something along the lines of "I have neither given nor received help on this assignment") and you do it. Then, if you break it, you're in trouble for violating the honor code. The getting-in-trouble part can lead to anything from facing a jury of your peers to sitting with your parents in the principal's office, at which point someone will bring up the value of the honor code.

Assuming you're like the majority of students, this might be your reaction to this system:

Why would writing a silly pledge be any more likely to make me not cheat? If I'm the kind of student who cheats, I'm probably also the kind of student who lies.

Good point.

Plus, my school has an honor code, and I still see people cheating all the time. What gives?

Also a good point.

YOU NEED TO KNOW: Traditional and Modified Honor Codes

The following definition from an interview with Donald McCabe, a prominent ressearcher, was reported by College Administration Publications (n.d.) and clarifies his investigations of honor codes:

> Strong traditional academic honor codes often include such provisions as unproctored exams, the use of some form of pledge that students are asked to sign attesting to the integrity of their work, and a strong (often exclusive) student role in the judicial system that addresses allegations of academic dishonesty. Some traditional codes also include provisions that encourage or require students to report any cheating they may see among other students.
>
> Modified honor code approaches typically include a strong or exclusive role for students in the judicial process but generally do not mandate unproctored exams or the use of a pledge, although they can often be used at an instructor's option in selected courses. What modified honor code approaches do, however, is place a strong campus focus on the issue of academic integrity. I believe this simple fact alone explains much of the success of modified honor codes. Students are reminded, often quite frequently, that their campus places a high value on the question of academic integrity. Policies are clearly communicated to students, and they are asked to personally exercise responsibility for academic integrity.

Here's the bottom line for schools: honor codes work, at least if you go by percentages. But do they work every time? No. The implementation of an honor code won't *eliminate* academic dishonesty, even if, statistically speaking, it reduces the frequency with which acts of dishonesty occur. The worst offenders will still cheat, while you (because we've already established that you're not a cheater) may bristle at having to write a disclaimer on every paper and test.

There is, however, a fairly slim margin of students whose conscience overcomes the temptation to cheat given a gentle nudge or those for whom a simple reminder may be enough to correct errors of process. Donald McCabe's research (summarized in an article titled "New Research on Academic Integrity" [College Administration Publications n.d.]) clearly demonstrates such improvements on college campuses (see Figure 5.1).

Note that, according to McCabe's research, cheating and plagiarism are still committed at some point by almost *one-half* of all students. Still, the effects of an honor code at the institutional level are clear; honor codes tend to reduce academic dishonesty from the school's point of view.

What does that mean for you? That's for you to decide. Either you make the pledge personal or it's just a bunch of words on paper. If your school doesn't have an honor code, that doesn't have to stop you from making a pledge to yourself. If you do it, chances are you'll stick to it. If you don't, you'll never know.

Serious Cheating on Campuses			
When	**Private Campuses with Honor Code**	**Large Public University with Modified Honor Code**	**Campuses with No Honor Code**
On tests	23 percent	33 percent	45 percent
On written work	45 percent	50 percent	56 percent

Figure 5.1

■ WRITE TO THE POINT

What are the elements of your personal honor code? What actions are acceptable and unacceptable as you complete your schoolwork? In the space below, make a short list or offer a brief explanation of the honor code you set for yourself.

_____

_____

_____

_____

My Classroom, My School

Each year my school holds an honor assembly, a gathering of all the students in our school auditorium. Students, not teachers, come to the stage to discuss aspects of the honor code and how they see them applying to real situations in the classroom. Then students are invited to sign an honor book that includes signatures of students collected over many years. The signing takes place behind a curtain, individually; students have the choice to sign or not to sign. Not signing the book does not release students from the honor code; rather, the choice to sign is presented as a possibility to make a personal commitment to integrity and honorable behavior.

In my own classroom, I don't require a pledge on student papers, though many teachers on campus do. Instead, I discuss citation and attribution before each and every major paper—both how to cite and *why*—and try to make the honor code work *for* students when possible. I sometimes trust the seniors I teach to take tests on their own, to make up in-class essays at home, or to bring their own notes into an exam. Do they cheat? Probably some do, but by discussing their practice, and what's right and wrong, *before* I make such assignments, I believe that I significantly cut down on cheating and plagiarism and build an expectation of maturity and professionalism that students respect.

Would an honor assembly make any difference to you personally or to your school as a whole? Do a teacher's expectations directly influence your decisions to cheat or not cheat? Why or why not?

Voices from the Classroom

The idea of having an all-knowing database of papers and words; it's almost invasive. It's much more effective to have just you and yourself and your conscience deciding what to do. The honor code provides a standard which we *should* all go by. If you don't abide by it, you eventually get screwed—later in life, just lacking the knowledge. Or getting caught and they bring up the violation of the honor code as a step toward getting kicked out of school—it's not worth it. In the short term, you get a personal gain from plagiarizing, but if you take the time to do it yourself, that's a long-term effect. But in a way and in theory the honor code discourages plagiarism; in reality, I don't think it does.

—*Antonio, age fourteen*

At the end of his comments, Antonio suggests that honor codes don't really work, however valuable they may be. What do you think? Does or would an honor code work for your school? Why or why not?

Team Efforts: Collaboration and Cheating

In 2007, the Duke University School of Business expelled, suspended, or failed more than thirty students (around 10 percent of the class of 2008) for cheating. The offense: collaborating on a take-home, open-book exam in violation of the school honor code. *BusinessWeek* (2007) commented on the scandal the next month:

> It's easy to imagine the explanations these MBAs, who are mulling an appeal, might come up with. Teaming up on a take-home exam: That's not academic fraud, it's postmodern learning, wiki style. Text-messaging exam answers or downloading essays onto iPods: That's simply a wise use of technology. . . . That's not to say that university administrators should ignore unethical behavior, if it in fact occurred. But in this wired world, maybe the very notion of what constitutes cheating has to be reevaluated.

And reader backlash against the *BusinessWeek* commentary was predictably full of outrage: cheating is cheating, readers insisted, and no matter how flat the world gets, individual accountability still stands for something.

Presbyterian Ladies' College (a K–12 school) in Australia, on the other hand, turned to this novel approach: instead of eliminating cheating through the use of cell phones, iPods, and email on exams, the school decided to allow any and all electronic devices in the name of a real-world style of testing. The testing style, which is being used only on timed assessments, is defended by some teachers, according to one article:

> Teachers say it is a better way to assess the online and verbal communication skills that students need to function in the modern world.
>
> The students themselves say having access to their phones and the internet did not make the assessment tasks any easier and tested their time management capabilities to the limit. (ABC News 2008)

In one assessment, students were required to write a sonnet. Some phoned family members, others looked up helpful sites online, and some did the work entirely on their own.

■ TALKING POINT

How often are you asked to complete work on your own that might be easier to complete or lead to more learning if completed through collaborative efforts? On the other hand, how often do students at your school collaborate when they shouldn't? Do teachers at your school ever build collaboration into the assignments they give and, if so, when and how? Do you enjoy or learn from such assignments differently than you learn from or enjoy working alone?

Few schools are poised to follow the example of Presbyterian Ladies' College. The Duke case, however, in which students were, on average, twenty-nine years old and generally experienced in the workplace and in education, raises even more profound questions for middle and high school. Imagine the mixed messages you might receive from teachers who mean well: Cooperation and teamwork are important, but I want to see what you can do on your own. Contribute to your group, but not too much. There's no excuse for grammatical errors in your essays—didn't you get someone to *proofread*?—but too much help on an essay is plagiarism.

Say, for example, a friend calls you with a question about homework; she doesn't understand some of the terms, even though the teacher explained them in class. Is it cheating for you to explain? What if it's vocabulary homework? Different teachers might have different answers, and so might different students.

You have to be careful about collaboration: follow the rules, share intelligently, and ask a teacher before you overstep any bounds that might lead to trouble later.

Get Cut, or Cut and Paste? Other Factors That May Influence Academic Honesty

If we look only at statistics, a worst-case scenario for any teacher is to see an overachieving male football player walk into the room.

Right. I can hear you, again:

Hey, wait just a minute! I know plenty of football players who make good grades. What's wrong with that?

Voices from the Classroom

By tenth grade, if you've been caught and there was a specific consequence, you learn a lesson. Past that point, most students know right from wrong. The first inclination, though, is to think that the older students are, the more mature they are and the less likely to cheat or plagiarize. But the younger kids are actually less likely to cheat—they still respect authority; their ideas of right and wrong are black and white. Older students develop a sense of arbitrariness and ask themselves, "Well, is it really wrong?" But remember, our brains aren't really fully developed until we reach our twenties, so the decision-making process for a teen is *not* what an adult thinks it should be. Expectations and consequences still matter for just that reason.

—*School counselor*

In your experience, do younger or older students tend to cheat and plagiarize more? Why do you think the trend happens in the way you've experienced?

Absolutely nothing, and I admit I was going for shock value. Remember, that scenario occurs if we look only at statistics. Studies show that football players cheat more than other athletes, that boys cheat more than girls, and that top-achieving and under-achieving students cheat more than those in the middle. But—and I emphasize this point—*you* are not a statistic, are you? And in every one of the cases I just mentioned, the statistics don't say that 100 percent of those students cheat—just that more do.

So what's your point?

Thanks for asking. My point is, again, that culture matters. Peer pressure is just one of the pressures school puts on you, but it's very real. And it's also true that within smaller cultural circles, you may be pressured to act in certain ways.

Take football players. First of all, it's important to point out that a survey of high school athletes reported by the Josephson Institute (2006a) reveals that the number of athletes who cheat (66 percent) is only slightly higher than the number of nonathletes who cheat (60 percent). With football players, the number goes up to 72 percent.

But I don't think football players cheat more because they play football, do you? It's more likely, I imagine, that it has to do with the amount of time they're asked to devote to the sport. In some schools, a particular culture may develop among closely bonded athletes that leads them to act appropriately or inappropriately, as well, whether those athletes play football or basketball or any other sport.

And the other statistics I mentioned? When asked, "How many times have you copied an Internet document for a classroom assignment in the past year?" by the Josephson Institute (2006b) in a survey titled "The Ethics of America's Youth," 40 percent of high school boys answered that they had done so at least once, compared with 26 percent of girls (the numbers for middle school: 28 percent and 19 percent, respectively). Most studies, though not all, back up this disparity.

Similarly, it's been widely reported that a 1998 survey by *Who's Who Among American High School Students* found that 80 percent of the "best of the nation's 16- to 18-year olds" cheated to get there (Goode 1999). It's also true, however, that underachieving students are more likely to plagiarize and cheat than other students, or, as a 1999 Educational Testing Service fact sheet puts it, "Students with lower GPA's or those at the very top" are most likely to cheat.

I repeat: you are not a statistic. The pressures that exist in schools are real, however, and I bring up these studies not to make you feel accused or guilty or as if cheating is inevitable because you play a sport or were born a male, but because recognizing that such pressures exist is a first step toward dealing with them in a mature manner.

Consider, for instance, these suggestions:

- *Be aware of the attitudes that surround you—and think about whether or not you agree.* It may be that everyone in your class thinks cheating is justified because the teacher is boring or because she grades harshly, or that copy-and-paste plagiarism is no big deal. Whether or not you agree with such attitudes is entirely up to you, but it's easy to fall into line with the way others think if you're not actively questioning those beliefs and attitudes.

- *Talk to the adults around you about cheating and plagiarism.* According to the Josephson Institute (2006a) report I cited earlier, 90 percent of athletes think coaches want them to do the right thing ethically "no matter what the cost." Sometimes adults, including parents, coaches, teachers, and administrators, view decisions differently from your peers, and it's worth seeking out those different viewpoints before you make up your own mind.

■ WRITE TO THE POINT

In the space below, describe any groups you're a part of within your school—sports teams, clubs, or other groupings. Do any of these groups have a culture or shared attitude that actively supports or does not support plagiarism or cheating? If so, why do you think that is? How do you deal with those attitudes when they arise?

_____

_____

_____

_____

_____

_____

_____

_____

_____

Final Thoughts: Being an Original, Not a Copy

There's one more case study left in this book for you to consider, but that's not the last time you'll run into stories about plagiarism. Your teachers probably all have several stories they could share. Plagiarism is in the news constantly; while I was working on this book, accusations of plagiarism plagued nominees for president and vice president, writers, and teachers, and those accusations were reported in the news across the nation and world. Plagiarism is a pervasive topic and challenge on college campuses, and it's becoming more and more of a sore subject with many professors and administrators.

Plagiarism won't go away, no matter how many students read copies of this book. As I said at the outset, plagiarism is easy, and anything that's easy is here to stay. But it's also certain that plagiarism is wrong, that you don't want to get caught engaging in it, and that when you plagiarize, you cheat yourself as much as others (that may sound trite, but it's true). At the start of this book, I told you that you need to be certain you can handle the temptations of plagiarism *before* you encounter them. I hope that by the end of this book you feel equipped to do so.

Early in this book, I offered a case study that involved Helen Keller's plagiarism as a young girl. That experience encouraged Keller to reflect on her task as a writer, as well, as she relates in the same chapter of her autobiography:

> Trying to write is very much like trying to put a Chinese puzzle together. We have a pattern in mind which we wish to work out in words; but the words will not fit the spaces, or, if they do, they will not match the design. But we keep on trying because we know that others have succeeded, and we are not willing to acknowledge defeat.
>
> "There is no way to become original, except to be born so," says Stevenson, and although I may not be original, I hope sometime to outgrow my artificial, periwigged compositions. Then, perhaps, my own thoughts and experiences will come to the surface. (1952, 68)

I believe that every student, every writer, has something original to say. Stevenson's comment is true, but one might also point out that if we aren't born originals, we also aren't born as plagiarists, though sometimes we make decisions that lead us in that direction. Writing is hard, as Keller suggests, but it's rewarding, and if you're not willing to acknowledge defeat, you just may find that avoiding plagiarism is no longer simply about avoiding consequences, but about searching for the original and valuable ideas you have to express.

■ CASE STUDY: FIGURES OF SPEECH

Here's a real news story with an interesting twist. It involves a 2008 high school graduation ceremony in Naperville, Illinois, at which it was discovered that the valedictorian had plagiarized his speech, lifting it from an article originally printed by the *Onion*:

> "We see these events as serious breaches of our standards and an aberration from the norm," [Superintendent] Leis said as he concluded a prepared statement. "When issues like these arise, it is very important that we reinforce the consistent expectation of ethical behavior." (WBBM780 2008)

After the valedictorian's plagiarism was discovered, he was asked to return his medal, and the speech was cut from the video of the commencement ceremony.

But here's the twist. In the same ceremony, the press soon reported, the principal of the high school had plagiarized *his* speech as well—this time from a former student, now a teacher at the school. One article reporting the incident offered this description of the principal's theft from the former student:

> He started tweaking her work. He says he planned to call her for permission but because it was late at night decided to ask her in person the next day.
>
> That conversation never happened. Caudill was busy that day and says it wasn't until midway through the speech that night that he realized his error. (Jenco 2008)

The case provoked some controversy among students and commentators; some thought the principal's mistake should be forgiven and others believed he should be fired.

In the same article from the *Daily Herald*, Superintendent Leis offered this opinion:

> "Administrators are held to even higher standards than teachers, and we can't in good honesty tell students it's wrong (to plagiarize) and then say it's OK for an administrator, any administrator."

In the end, the principal was moved to another position in the system the next year.

Find Out More

Locate the articles cited in this case study or do a web search for this plagiarism case to read more about the situation. As you read, look for any information that might change the way you feel about the actions of the principal and the valedictorian or the reactions of others.

Talking Points

1. Do you believe the consequences faced by the valedictorian and the principal were fair? Should either have faced more or less severe consequences than he did?

2. Does the principal's explanation of the steps that led him to plagiarize change your opinion about his actions or the consequences he faced?

3. What external pressures combined to lead these two different speakers to plagiarize their remarks? How else might they have eased those pressures? Might those pressures have been enough to cause them to act out of character in this one instance?

Appendix
A Guide to Basic Citation in MLA and APA Styles

MLA	APA
BOOKS	
Book with one author (basic, later edition, with editors)	
Copy, Ivana. <u>Title of Book</u>. Place of Publication: Publisher, Year of Publication.	League, I. V. (Year of Publication). <u>Title of Book</u>. Place of Publication: Publisher.
Copy, Ivana. <u>Title of Book</u>. 2nd ed. Place of Publication: Publisher, Year of Publication.	League, I. V. (Year of Publication). <u>Title of Book</u> (2nd ed). Place of Publication: Publisher.
Copy, Ivana and Bea Careful, eds. <u>Title of Book</u>. Place of Publication: Publisher, Year of Publication.	League, I. V., and Afterschool, C.U. (Eds.). (Year of Publication). <u>Title of Book</u>. Place of Publication: Publisher.
Book with multiple authors	
Copy, Ivana and Bea Careful. <u>Title of Book</u>. Place of Publication: Publisher, Year of Publication.	League, I. V., & Afterschool, C. U. (Year of Publication). <u>Title of Book</u>. Place of Publication: Publisher.
Multiple books by one author	
Copy, Ivana. <u>First Title of Book</u>. Place of Publication: Publisher, Year of Publication. ———. <u>Second Title of Book</u>. Place of Publication: Publisher, Year of Publication.	League, I. V. (Earlier Year of Publication). <u>Title of Book</u>. Place of Publication: Publisher. League, I. V. (Later Year of Publication). <u>Title of Book</u>. Place of Publication: Publisher.
Book by a corporate author (e.g., a book by Beekeepers International with no author)	
Group Name. <u>Title of Book</u>. Place of Publication: Publisher, Year of Publication.	Group Name. (Year of Publication). <u>Title of Book</u>. Place of Publication: Publisher.
Poem or short story within a collection or anthology	
Careful, Bea. "Poem Title." <u>Book Title</u>. Ed. Ivana Copy. Publication Place: Publisher, Date of Publication. Page Number.	Poet, Ima. (Year of Publication). Title of Poem. In I. V. League (Ed.), <u>Title of Book</u> (Page Numbers). Place of Publication: Publisher.
Introduction, preface, or afterword (first name = author of introduction, second name = author/editor of entire book)	
Copy, Ivana. Introduction. <u>Title of Book</u>. By Bea Careful. Place of Publication: Publisher, Year of Publication. Page Numbers.	League, I. V. (Year of Publication). Introduction. In Afterschool, C.U. (Ed.), <u>Title of Book</u> (Page Numbers). Place of Publication: Publisher.

MLA	APA
PERIODICALS (ARTICLES)	
Article in a magazine	
Copy, Ivana. "Title of Article." <u>Title of Periodical</u> Day Month Year: pages.	League, I. V. (Year of Publication). Title of Article. <u>Title of Periodical,</u> volume number, page numbers.
Newspaper article	
Copy, Ivana. "Title of Article." <u>Title of Newspaper</u> Day Month Year: edition.	League, I. V. (Year of Publication, Date of Publication). Title of Article. <u>Title of Newspaper,</u> page numbers.
Anonymous articles	
"Title of Article." <u>Title of Periodical</u> Day Month Year: pages.	Title of Article. (Year of Publication, Date of Publication). <u>Title of Newspaper,</u> page numbers.
ELECTRONIC SOURCES	
An entire website	
<u>Name of Site</u>. Date of Posting/Revision. Name of Site Host. Date Site was Accessed <URL>.	League, I. V. (Year of Publication, Date of Publication). <u>Title of Website.</u> Retrieved Date of Access, from URL.
A single webpage	
Copy, Ivana. "Title of Web Page." <u>Name of Site</u>. Date of Posting/Revision. Name of Site Host. Date Site was Accessed <URL>.	League, I. V. (Year of Publication, Date of Publication). Title of Web Page. <u>Title of Website.</u> Retrieved Date of Access, from URL.
An online article (from a magazine or journal)	
Copy, Ivana. "Title of Article." <u>Title of Online Publication</u>. Date of Publication. Date of Access <electronic address>.	League, I. V. (Year of Publication). Title of Article [Electronic version]. <u>Title of Periodical,</u> volume number, page numbers.
A blog posting	
Last Name, First. "Title of Entry." Weblog Entry. Title of Weblog. Date Posted. Date Accessed <URL>.	League, I. V. (Year of Publication). Title of Entry. Title of Weblog: I.V. League's Weblog. Retrieved Date and Year from URL.
IN-TEXT CITATIONS	
Author page (no comma)	Author date (with comma)
The author suggests that "plagiarism is bad—really bad" (Copy 73).	The author believes that "plagiarism may cause the common cold" (Afterschool, 2007, p. 39).
Copy suggests that "plagiarism is bad" and may "lead to severe consequences" (73).	C. U. Afterschool (2007) warns that "plagiarism makes you feel even worse than the sniffles" (p. 39).

Works Cited

Case Study: Blind Justice?

Keller, Helen. 1952. *The Story of My Life*. Garden City, NJ: Doubleday.

Schleicher, Annie. 2006. "Plagiarism Scandal Exposes World of Book Packaging." *Newshour Extra*. www.pbs.org/newshour/extra/features/jan-june06/author_5-03.html (accessed Aug. 29, 2008).

Zeller, Tom Jr. 2006. "In Internet Age, Writers Face Frontier Justice." *New York Times*, May 1. www.nytimes.com/2006/05/01/business/media/01link.html?_r=1&th&emc=th&oref=slogin (accessed Feb. 8, 2008).

Chapter 2: Copies (and Robberies)

Burg, Barbara, et al. 2007. *Writing with Internet Sources: A Guide for Harvard Students*. Cambridge: Expository Writing Program, Harvard College.

Campbell, Don. 2007. "The Plagiarism Plague." *National Crosstalk*. www.highereducation.org/crosstalk/ct0106/news0106-plagiarism.shtml (accessed Feb. 18, 2008).

Clabaugh, Gary K., and Edward G. Rozycki. 2003. "Defining Plagiarism." In *Preventing Cheating and Plagiarism*, 2d ed. Oreland, PA: NewFoundations. www.newfoundations.com/PREVPLAGWEB/DefiningPlagiarism.html (accessed Feb. 19, 2008).

College Administration Publications. n.d. "New Research on Academic Integrity: The Success of 'Modified' Honor Codes." www.collegepubs.com/ref/SFX000515.shtml (accessed Mar. 23, 2008).

Cope, Virginia H. 1995. "Mark Twain's Huckleberry Finn: Text, Illustrations, and Early Reviews." University of Virginia. http://etext.virginia.edu/twain/huckfinn.html (accessed Feb. 18, 2008).

iParadigms. 2007. "Did You Know?" Plagiarism.org. www.plagiarism.org/learning_center/did_you_know.html (accessed Feb. 18, 2008).

———. 2008. Turnitin.com. www.turnitin.com/ (accessed Feb. 10, 2008).

Martin, Melissa, and Stephanie Martin. n.d. "SparkNote on *The Adventures of Huckleberry Finn*." www.sparknotes.com/lit.huckfin (accessed Feb. 18, 2008).

Meyer, Michael. 1993. *The Bedford Introduction to Literature*. 3d ed. Boston: Bedford Books.

Muha, Dave. 2003. "New Study Confirms Internet Plagiarism Is Prevalent." Office of Media Relations, Rutgers University. Aug. 28. http://ur.rutgers.edu/medrel/viewArticle.html?ArticleID=3408 (accessed Feb. 19, 2008).

123helpme.com. n.d. "Free Essays—Survival in *The Adventures of Huckleberry Finn*." www.123helpme.com/view.asp?id=16713 (accessed Feb. 18, 2008).

U.S. National Library of Medicine. 2008. "Sickle-Cell Anemia." Medline Plus. Mar. 14. www.nlm.nih.gov/medlineplus/sicklecellanemia.html (accessed Mar. 19, 2008).

Wikipedia contributors. 2008. "Sickle-Cell Disease." Wikipedia. Mar. 18. http://en.wikipedia.org/wiki/Sickle-cell_disease (accessed Mar. 19, 2008).

Case Study: Take It or Leave It

CBS. 2002. "Cheating in the Heartland?" *48 Hours*, May 31. www.cbsnews.com/stories/2002/05/31/48hours/main510772.shtml (accessed Feb. 20, 2008).

Chapter 3: Write from Wrong

Go, Alison. 2008. "Two Students Kicked off Semester at Sea for Plagiarism." *U.S. News and World Report*. www.usnews.com/blogs/paper-trail/2008/8/14/two-students-kicked-off-semester-at-sea-for-plagiarism.html (accessed Aug. 29, 2008).

Goldberg, Carey. 2006. "Have You Ever Plagiarized? If So, You're in Good Company." *Boston Globe*, May 1. www.boston.com/news/globe/health_science/articles/2006/05/01/have_you_ever_plagiarized_if_so_youre_in_good_company/?page=1 (accessed Feb. 22, 2008).

Sampson, Zinie Chen. 2008. "Students Expelled from U.Va. Shipboard Program for Plagiarism." PilotOnline.com. Aug. 11. http://hamptonroads.com/2008/08/students-expelled-uva-shipboard-program-plagiarism (accessed Aug. 29, 2008).

Schworm, Peter. 2008. "College Applications Can Be Too Good." *Boston Globe*, Feb. 12. www.boston.com/news/education/higher/articles/2008/02/12/college_applications_can_be_too_good/ (accessed Feb. 25, 2008).

Chapter 4: Copy That!

Gilmore, Barry. 2007. *"Is It Done Yet?": Teaching Adolescents the Art of Revision.* Portsmouth, NH: Heinemann.

Guinee, Kathleen, and Maya B. Eagleton. 2006. "Spinning Straw into Gold: Transforming Information into Knowledge During Web-Based Research." *English Journal* 95: 46–52.

Harris, Robert. 2007. "Evaluating Internet Research Sources." Virtualsalt. June 15. www.virtualsalt.com/evalu8it.htm (accessed Mar. 23, 2008).

Lester, James D. 2004. *Writing Research Papers: A Complete Guide.* New York: Longman.

Chapter 5: Making It Personal

ABC News. 2008. "School Takes Modern Approach to Student Exams." www.abc.net.au/news/stories/2008/08/20/2341657.htm (accessed Aug. 29, 2008).

American Psychological Association (APA). 1998. "Research Shows Homework Does Boost Academic Achievement; but Overemphasizing Grades and Performance May Lead to Cheating." *ScienceDaily,* Mar. 4. www.sciencedaily.com/releases/1998/03/980304073520.htm (accessed Mar. 23, 2008).

BusinessWeek. 2007. "Cheating—or Postmodern Learning?" May 14. www.businessweek.com/magazine/content/07_20/b4034056.htm (accessed Mar. 23, 2008).

College Administration Publications. n.d. "New Research on Academic Integrity: The Success of 'Modified' Honor Codes." www.collegepubs.com/ref/SFX000515.shtml (accessed Mar. 23, 2008).

Educational Testing Service. 1999. "Academic Cheating Fact Sheet." www.glass-castle.com/clients/www-nocheating-org/adcouncil/research/ (accessed Aug. 29, 2008).

Goode, Stephen. 1999. "Students Get A+ for Easy Cheating." Insight on the News. http://findarticles.com/p/articles/mi_m1571/is_35_15/ai_55927016 (accessed Mar. 23, 2008).

The Josephson Institute. 2006a. "Are Coaches Teaching Our Young Athletes the Right Way to Play?" http:// josephsoninstitute.org/sports/programs/survey/index.html (accessed Mar. 23, 2008).

———. 2006b. "The Ethics of American Youth." http://charactercounts .org/programs/reportcard/2006/data-tables.html (accessed Mar. 23, 2008).

Keller, Helen. 1952. *The Story of My Life.* Garden City, NJ: Doubleday.

Kellogg, Alex P. 2002. "Students Plagiarize Less than Many Think, a New Study Finds." *Chronicle of Higher Education.* http://chronicle.com/free/2002/02/2002020101t.htm (accessed Mar. 23, 2008).

Case Study: Figures of Speech

Jenco, Melissa. 2008. "Naperville Central Principal May Be Reassigned After Plagiarism Flap." *The Daily Herald.* www.dailyherald.com/story/?id=199940 (accessed Aug. 29, 2008).

WBBM 780. 2008. "Plagiarism Plagues Naperville Central, Principal and Valedictorian Busted." www.wbbm780.com/pages/2275810.php? (accessed Aug. 29, 2008).

Index